National Industrial Policy

About the Editors

WILLIAM F. CLINGER is a Republican representing Pennsylvania's 23rd District and is serving his third term in the U.S. House of Representatives. He is Chairman of the House Wednesday Group and serves on the Public Works and Transportation Committee where he is ranking member of the Economic Development Subcommittee. Congressman Clinger also formerly served as the Chief Counsel to the Economic Development Administration and is the author of numerous magazine and newspaper articles on economic development.

NANCY L. JOHNSON is a Republican representing Connecticut's 6th District and is serving her first term in the U.S. House of Representatives. She is a member of the House Committee on Public Works and Transportation, the Committee on Veterans Affairs, and the Select Committee on Children, Youth, and Families. Congresswoman Johnson also serves on the House Republican Research Committee's Export Task Force and is a member of the Steering Committee of the House Republican Research Committee's Task Force on High Tech Initiatives. She formerly served in Connecticut's State Legislature from 1977 to 1982.

LYNN MARTIN is a Republican representing Illinois' 16th District and is serving her second term in the U.S. House of Representatives. She serves on the Budget Committee and the Public Works and Transportation Committee and is also a member of the Export Task Force, the Congressional Rural Caucus and serves on the Steering Committee for the Northeast-Midwest Congressional Coalition. Congresswoman Martin is a member of the Republican Policy Committee, and she formerly served in the Illinois State Legislature both as a State Senator and as a State Representative.

THOMAS E. PETRI is a Republican representing Wisconsin's 6th District and is serving his third term in the U.S. House of Representatives. He is a member of the House Education and Labor Committee and is the ranking Republican on the House Human Resources Subcommittee. Mr. Petri also serves on the House Public Works and Transportation Committee. In his varied career before his election to Congress, Mr. Petri was a Peace Corps Volunteer in Somalia, a White House aide and a state senator.

National Industrial Policy
Solution or Illusion

edited by
Thomas E. Petri,
William F. Clinger, Jr.,
Nancy L. Johnson,
and Lynn Martin

Westview Press / Boulder & London

A *Westview Special Study*

All rights reserved. No part of this publication may be reproduced or transmitted in any form or by any means, electronic or mechanical, including photocopy, recording, or any information storage and retrieval system, without permission in writing from the publisher.

Copyright © 1984 by Westview Press, Inc.

Published in 1984 in the United States of America by
    Westview Press, Inc.
    5500 Central Avenue
    Boulder, Colorado 80301
    Frederick A. Praeger, Publisher

ISBN 0-8133-7028-0

Composition for this book was provided by the editors.
Printed and bound in the United States of America.

10 9 8 7 6 5 4 3 2

Contents

Acknowledgments	ix
Introduction, THOMAS E. PETRI	1

CHAPTER ONE
    THE DEBATE DEFINED
    Overview, WILLIAM F. CLINGER,JR, ... 3

    Industrial Policy: A Dissent, CHARLES L. SCHULTZE . 7
    Fashionable Myths of National Industrial Policy,
    RICHARD B. McKENZIE 27

CHAPTER TWO
    THE LESSONS OF EXPERIENCE
    Overview, NANCY L. JOHNSON 49

    Industrial Policy in Japan, PHILIP H. TREZISE . . . 53
    West Germany: Another Industrial Policy Victim,
    KLAUS-DIETER SCHMIDT 63
    Britain's Industrial Policy: Valuable Lessons for
    the U.S., JOHN BURTON 71
    Industrial Innovation Policy: Lessons from American
    History, RICHARD R. NELSON and RICHARD N. LANGLOIS. 85

CHAPTER THREE
    CHANGING ECONOMIC STRUCTURE
    Overview, LYNN MARTIN 97

    The Myth of U.S. Deindustrialization,
    ROBERT Z. LAWRENCE 101
    The Myth of Deindustrialization, WILLIAM BRANSON . . 115
    Manufacturing: Meeting the Global Competition,
    PAT CHOATE 125

CHAPTER FOUR
    POLICY RECOMMENDATIONS
        Overview, THOMAS E. PETRI 133

        How To Improve the Competitiveness of American
        Industry, JOHN A. YOUNG 139
        Strategy for U.S. Industrial Competitiveness,
        COMMITTEE FOR ECONOMIC DEVELOPMENT 147

Conclusion, THOMAS E. PETRI, WILLIAM F. CLINGER, JR.,
    NANCY L. JOHNSON, LYNN MARTIN 159
Contributors 163
Bibliography 165
Index 171

Acknowledgments

A noted author once observed: "A book is the last link in a chain of links. If any one of them break along the way, the book would not be written." This is particularly so in the case of this book.

We are especially grateful to Alfred M. Randolf, Jr. of the House Wednesday Group staff for his assistance in coordinating the overall project. This book could not have been completed without his patience and hard work.

We are also grateful to Louise Gobron of the House Wednesday Group staff for her exhaustive research in support of the special debate that spawned this book. In addition, we would like to thank Joe Flader, Howard Bomberg, Matt Cook and Fran McNaught for their assistance in reviewing specific chapters, and Gretchen Pagel, Ted Van Der Meid, Ben Cohen, Tina Clarke, Peter Mayers, Lori Tansey and Susie Roberts for their general editorial assistance.

Tom Petri
Bill Clinger
Nancy Johnson
Lynn Martin

Introduction

Thomas E. Petri

National Industrial Policy is a catchy phrase. Like many catchy phrases, it has become a popular subject of discussion in the United States and abroad. It has also appeared politically useful in some quarters, since it conjures up images of vital manufacturing industries in dire peril and government (i.e., politicians) riding to the rescue with dramatic "new ideas."

Catchy phrases with broad political programs attached should be subject to careful analysis. In the first place, what does the phrase itself mean? Industrial policy COULD mean any government involvement in the economy intended to promote industry, including fiscal and monetary policy, trade policy, tax policy, anti-trust, education programs, regulation, and others. All of these items which establish the broad structure of incentives in the economy are important, but they are not really what the national industrial policy debate is about. The debate is about a more specific set of actions to address a particular perceived problem.

The problem is the supposed "deindustrialization" of America—an alleged inability to compete internationally in basic manufacturing industries such as steel, autos, and machine tools, together with a danger that we will be left behind in emerging "high tech" industries as well. The two key solutions are some kind of tripartite national planning agency, bringing together representatives of industry, labor and government to direct the economy; and a government investment bank to channel capital to favored industries and firms. A national industrial policy is then the targeting of particular industries and firms for special help by a planning agency and a bank. As it turns out, the problem does not really exist, and if it did, the solutions would only make it worse, but that is getting ahead of our story.

The idea for this book came out of a special debate on the subject of industrial policy which was held on November 17, 1983, in the U.S. House of Representatives. Fifteen members of Congress participated in an effort to examine this complex issue thoroughly

1

and insert in the Congressional Record articles on the subject by leading economists of all political persuasions. The results of this debate were so illuminating—particularly the almost uniform rejection of industrial policy by the expert community—that four of us have decided to organize the best material we have seen on the subject and present it to a wider audience in the form of this book.

The book contains four chapters. The first, "The Debate Defined," edited by Congressman Bill Clinger, presents two of the finest theoretical discussions of the entire issue.

The lessons of the past can be an important guide for the future. Chapter Two, "The Lessons of Experience," edited by Congresswoman Nancy Johnson, recounts the experiences of several nations, including our own, with the kinds of institutions and programs proposed by industrial policy advocates.

Chapter Three, "Changing Economic Structure," edited by Congresswoman Lynn Martin, examines many of the assumptions that underlie the call for a national industrial policy, and enables us to evaluate carefully the need for such a policy.

Finally, Chapter Four, "Policy Recommendations," surveys specific suggestions of what business, government, and labor should do, apart from industrial policy, to improve the performance of our economy.

We hope this book presents sufficient facts and analysis to enable concerned citizens to cut through the rhetoric surrounding this issue and make up their own minds about the usefulness of industrial policy. At this time, industrial policy is only a theory on how to manage the economy. Political winds can change, however, and today's theory can become tomorrow's reality. The American people should know what such a change can mean.

CHAPTER ONE:
THE DEBATE DEFINED

Overview

William F. Clinger, Jr.

The term "industrial policy" has come to mean a particular set of policies to address a supposed lack of competitiveness in the American economy. Yet, in order to truly understand this term and its ramifications, we need to ask a few basic questions. First, what are the assumptions about the current economic situation which lead to the conclusion that we need an industrial policy? What constitutes an industrial policy? How should one be implemented? How valuable would such a policy be? Lastly, to what extent is one advisable?

In this first chapter, Charles Schultze, a senior fellow at the Brookings Institution and former chairman of the Council of Economic Advisers during the Carter Administration, and Richard McKenzie, a professor of economics at Clemson University and an adjunct scholar at the Heritage Foundation, address these questions and take a close look at the debate now raging over how government can best promote industrial competitiveness. Despite representing substantially different perspectives on virtually all other economic policy questions both authors oppose the formation of any national body to direct the nation's economy, and even question the claim that America is deindustrializing.

In his article, Schultze challenges each of the four premises underlying pro-industrial policy rhetoric. He argues "1. America is NOT deindustrializing; 2. Japan does NOT owe its industrial success to its industrial policy; 3. Government is NOT able to devise a 'winning' industrial structure; 4. It is NOT possible in the American political system to pick and choose among individual firms and regions in the substantive, efficiency-driven way envisaged by advocates of industrial policy." As a result, he explicitly rejects the need for what some call a new Reconstruction Finance Corporation, or what the most recent Democratic Party Platform calls an Economic Cooperation Council.

As Schultze notes, the very notion of a national industrial policy typically implies "picking winners and protecting losers." At the same time, Schultze warns that "we actually know precious little about identifying, before the fact, a 'winning' industrial structure." Moreover, precedent shows that federal handouts often go to the groups with the most clout in Washington rather than to those with the greatest need. As Schultze astutely observes, "those with the loudest squeak" are the ones who "get the grease."

While Schultze rejects industrial policy as the wrong solution to a non-existent problem, he does not deny that the U.S. has a number of real economic problems that require policy reforms. He points out that "we—along with every other industrial country—will have to walk a very fine line to sustain an economic recovery vigorous enough to make substantial inroads on unemployment, but not so buoyant as to risk a resurgence of inflationary pressures or inflationary expectations." He further observes that our most immediate problems are macroeconomic in nature, and that "getting America's monetary and fiscal policies in order is far more important for the health of the nation's industrial structure than any conceivable set of new industrial policies."

In his article, Richard McKenzie further defines the lines of debate by seeking to dispel what he refers to as the "fashionable myths of industrial policy." Among these he includes: "The manufacturing sector in the United States is on the wane...The country's employment base is rapidly changing...The federal government saved Chrysler from bankruptcy...Low wages in foreign countries explain the inability of U.S. industries to compete with imports."

Addressing those who predict the demise of America's manufacturing sector, McKenzie offers evidence that recent U.S. industrial problems are a natural although unfortunate consequence of the business cycle, not a long-term downward trend. He then goes on to say that the dynamic nature of the global economy is a reality that U.S. industry should exploit rather than resist. He observes that as some markets contract, others naturally expand, and that propping up "sunset" firms with large amounts of taxpayers' money only serves to upset the process by retarding the growth of "sunrise" firms, limiting incentives for industrial expansion and innovation, and adding to the never-ending increases in unnecessary government spending.

In response to those who support trade protection as part of America's industrial policy, McKenzie argues that "the honest slogan of the...protectionist...should probably be 'Buy American, Save Our Jobs, and Impose the Cost on Others." He then explains that the bidirectional nature of world trade makes an open market advantageous to both importers and exporters. The American purchase of foreign goods gives foreign markets—particularly those in the Third World—the capital needed to buy American-produced goods and services. This results in a more equitable balance of trade, and in a more developed global economy. Import restrictions would only lead to a devaluation of foreign currencies and an unfavorable position for American products manufactured for export. As McKenzie concludes, imports "create jobs in other export sectors of the U.S. economy, a fact that those who seek protection from market competition fail to acknowledge."

Government intervention in the private sector's industrial future seems necessary to some but misguided to others. Whether government should retain and embellish its role as a catalyst to market forces or whether it should expand this role to the point of becoming a SUBSTITUTE for market forces remains to be answered. Both Schultze and McKenzie champion the free market approach to America's industrial future and warn against near-sighted federal meddling in the free market structure. Both further agree that a nationally directed industrial policy would likely impede industrial growth, REDUCE overall U.S. industrial competitiveness, and misdirect the allocation of future U.S. economic resources. We should heed their warning and share their concern that the ambitious dream of national industrial planning could not only be an illusion but a harmful solution.

Industrial Policy:
A Dissent

Charles L. Schultze

The last ten years have been a time of troubles for most of the world's industrial economies. The growth of output and productivity has slowed. Both inflation and unemployment have averaged substantially higher than in earlier postwar years. And the decade has produced the two worst recessions of the postwar period.

In the United States, this experience has spawned two new economic doctrines, each purporting to explain the source of at least some of our economic ills and offering a plan of action to deal with them. These economic theories originated outside the mainstream of professional economic thought. The first of them is supply-side economics, which is based on a vast exaggeration of the incentive effects of lower taxes. It has had a spectacular political success, and was installed in early 1981 as official U.S. government policy.

The second of these new theories—and the latest entry into the competition for the hearts and minds of political candidates—is a set of economic ideas and policy recommendations that goes by the name "industrial policy." It has been the subject of a growing stream of books and articles; it has been endorsed as a concept by the AFL-CIO; its precepts have been incorporated in a number of bills now before the Congress; and it is receiving a sympathetic hearing from many of the candidates for the 1984 Democratic presidential nomination.

The phrase "industrial policy" means somewhat different things to different people; it refers not so much to a single theory as to a loose collection of similar diagnoses and proposals. The diagnoses generally cluster around two basic propositions:

FIRST, THE UNITED STATES HAS BEEN "DEINDUSTRIALIZING." The share of national output generated by manufacturing has been falling in recent years while the share attributable to services has been growing. Within manufacturing a number of essential heavy industries are in absolute decline, and the United States is no longer at the cutting edge of technological advance in the newer, high-tech industries. We are becoming increasingly uncompetitive in world markets. These are the symptoms of deep-seated structural problems; they will not be cured by macroeconomic measures aimed at overall economic growth. The private market is not directing investment to the right places; older manufacturing industries cannot find the funds they need to rehabilitate themselves, and promising new firms in the advancing sectors are often unable to secure as much venture capital as they need for growth. American labor makes it difficult to make the necesssary transition from older, declining industries to newer ones with good growth potential and high value-added per worker; this is partly because investment is being directed to the wrong industries and partly because laid-off workers do not have the skills needed or are not in the right locations. And when these dislocated workers eventually do get reemployed it is too often in low-skill jobs paying low wages. We are in danger of becoming a nation of hamburger joints and boutique shops.

SECOND, SOME OTHER COUNTRIES--JAPAN BEING THE PREEMINENT EXAMPLE--HAVE DEVELOPED GOVERNMENTAL POLICIES THAT SUCCESSFULLY PROMOTE VIGOROUS INDUSTRIAL GROWTH. The Japanese government identifies potential winners in the competition for world markets and encourages their growth, while simultaneously protecting and easing the burden of adjustment for older but essential heavy industries. Farsighted officials in the Japanese Ministry of International Trade and Industry (MITI), working closely with cooperative Japanese business leaders and bankers, plan and organize years in advance, such industrial achievements as the penetration of world automobile markets, the development of automated steel mills producing at water's edge for exports, the 256K memory chip, and now the ultimate super computer.

The various proponents of industrial policy offer a wide range of suggestions to deal with the industrial problems they identify. Many of their proposals involve new or modified federal initiatives in traditional areas: expanded support for technical education; research and development; and programs to retrain workers. Whatever the merits of these ideas, they do not constitute a major new thrust in economic policy. What is new, however, is the proposal that government deliberately set out to plan and create an industrial structure, and a pattern of output and investment significantly different from what the market would have produced. Two leading advocates of industrial policy, Ira Magaziner and Robert Reich, put the matter this way: "We suggest that U.S. companies and the government develop a coherent and coordinated industrial policy whose aim is to raise the real income of our citizens by improving the patterns of our investments rather than by focusing on only aggregate investment levels."[1]

Industrial policy thus aims to channel the flow of private investment towards some firms and industries--and necessarily, therefore, away from others. The government develops, at least in broad outline, an explicit conception of the direction in which industrial structure ought to be evolving, and then adopts a set of tax, loan, trade, regulatory, and other policies to lead economic activity along the desired path.

Industrial policy typically has two aspects--"picking the winners" and "protecting the losers"--and proponents sometimes disagree as to the relative emphasis to be placed on each. "Picking the winners" involves identifying industries that are at the cutting edge of economic progress, with such characteristics as high growth potential and high value-added per worker, and then providing investment subsidies, research support, and other assistance to existing firms and new entrants in those industries. "Protecting the losers," on the other hand, involves supporting and presumably helping to rehabilitate major declining industries. The government measures that would be deployed for this purpose include creation of barriers against competition from imports, special tax breaks, subsidized loans, and selectively favorable regulatory treatment. In most versions of industrial policy, the government, in a switch from current practice, would require that labor and management in these declining industries accept major reforms--wage restraint, reduction of feather-bedding rules, and improved managerial practices as preconditions for assistance.

In addition to the two explicit propositions noted above--that America has been de-industrializing and that the government of Japan has successfully managed industrial adjustment--there are two IMPLICIT premises on which the case for a U.S. industrial policy rests. The first of these is that the government has the analytical capabililty to determine with greater success than market forces what industrial structure is appropriate, who the potential winners are, which of the losers should be saved, and how they should be restructured. The second is that the American political system would (or could) make such critical choices among firms, individuals, and regions on the basis of economic criteria rather than political pressures.

In fact, as we shall see, reality does not square with any of the four premises on which the advocates of industrial policy rest their case. America is NOT de-industrializing. Japan does NOT owe its industrial success to its industrial policy. Government is NOT able to devise a "winning" industrial structure. Finally, it is NOT possible in the American political system to pick and choose among individual firms and regions in the substantive efficiency-driven way envisaged by advocates of industrial policy.

DE-INDUSTRIALIZATION: A NONEXISTENT TREND

America has not been de-industrializing. Throughout the industrial world, economic performance in the 1970s did fall behind the record of the 1960s. But relative to the industries of other countries, American industry performed quite well by almost all standards.[2]

During the decade of the 1970s, before the current recession began, the United States was vastly superior to the major European countries and to Japan in the generation of new jobs. Total employement grew by 24 percent in the United States during that decade. The next best performer was Japan, with a nine percent increase. Other countries were far behind; in Germany, for example, employment actually fell. Moreover, the United States was one of only three major industrial countries--Italy and Canada having been the others--with any increase in MANUFACTURING employment. According to OECD data, manufacturing production in in the United States, while rising less rapidly than production in Japan, grew faster than the European average and outstripped the gains made in Germany, a country that is usually mentioned, along with Japan, as a leading example of industrial strength.³

Manufacturing production in the United States typically rises more in business cycle expansions, and falls further in contractions, than does total GNP. After adjustment for this regular cyclical pattern--and contrary to popular impression--the share of private domestic GNP produced by manufacturing industries did not decline significantly in the 1970s.⁴ The proportion of total U.S. employment accounted for by manufacturing has been falling throughout the postwar period, but this principally reflects the fact that productivity growth (output per person) has continued to grow faster in manufacturing than in most other parts of the economy.

The relatively good performance of the industrial sector in the 1970s was partly due to a very large increase during the decade--in fact, a doubling--in exports of American manufactured goods. This was a good bit less than the rise in Japanese exports, but substantially higher than the increase experienced by Europe. America's export strength was aided by a decline in the real exchange value of the dollar, from an overvalued level at the beginning of the decade to what many people believed was a somewhat undervalued level at the end. Since it is unlikely that the value of the dollar will fall steadily over the long run, the share of U.S. economic activity accounted for by the manufacturing sector could conceivably decline very slowly. That would be a natural development, however, in no way reflecting a structural malaise requiring new governmental policies.

The United States does have some old-line heavy industries with deep-seated structural problems--especially the steel and automobile industries. But they are not typical of American industry generally. There is no evidence that in periods of reasonably normal prosperity American labor and capital are incapable of making the gradual transitions that are always required in a dynamic economy, as demand and output shift from older industries to newer ones at the forefront of technological advances.

Indeed, American industry successfully made some important and desirable structural adjustments in the 1970s, even though that was a decade of economic difficulties throughout the world. Thus, Robert Lawrence of Brookings reports that the U.S. international trade SURPLUS in the products of high-tech industries grew from $12 billion in 1972 to $40 billion in 1979, while the trade DEFICIT in other manufactured products rose from $15 billion to $35 billion in the same period. Yet, according to a study done for the National Commission for Employment Policy, dislocated workers--defined as unemployed people whose last jobs were in declining industries who had been out of work for more than eight weeks -- amounted to only 0.4 percent of the labor force in March, 1980.[5] In addition, although the total unemployment rate was higher in the United States than in most large European countries as the 1970s drew to a close, long-term unemployment was substantially lower.[6]

But even if it is true that the United States was not de-industrializing in the 1970s, has not the industrial sector performed very much worse than the economy in general during the past several years? Yes, it has. From 1981 through the fourth quarter of 1982--the trough of the recession--GNP declined by 2.2 percent while manufacturing production fell by 10.6 percent. But the outsized drop in manufacturing production occurred for two reasons having nothing to do with de-industrialization. First, as noted above, manufacturing production ALWAYS falls faster than GNP during recessions, and rises faster during booms. In the first half of 1983, for example, as GNP began to recover at a 5.9 percent annual rate, manufacturing production jumped up at an 16.2 percent rate. Second, the huge rise in the real exchange value of the dollar over the last two years discouraged U.S. exports and encouraged foreign imports--a development that had an especially depressing effect on American manufacturing industries. But the overvaluation of the dollar was obviously not caused by structural deficiencies of American industry; it was principally the result of the combination of tight money and loose budgetary policy that gave us unprecedentedly high interest rates. What is needed is a better mix of macroeconomic policies, not a new government agency to influence the pattern of industrial investment.

What about the dramatic fall in the rate of productivity growth in the United States during the 1970s? Does that not reflect, at least in part, a major structural problem in U.S. manufacturing sector? The pace of productivity growth did, indeed, decrease. While the reasons for this decline are still something of a mystery, a few things are known. First, the decline was worldwide--and its magnitude in the United States was about midway down the list of industrial countries. Second, the decline was not concentrated in manufacturing industries; in fact by most estimates it was somewhat smaller there than in the other sectors of the economy, and productivity growth has continued to be higher in manufacturing than in most sectors. Third, the decline was not caused by a shift in production away from high productivity manufacturing industries to low-productivity service industries.[7]

Productivity growth is the source of rising living standards. The sharp decline in that growth, in manufacturing and elsewhere, is the most serious long-run problem facing the U.S. economy. But there is no evidence that this decline stems from a tendency for the private market system to allocate investment to the "wrong" places--away from the manufacturing sector or, within manufacturing, to the wrong firms or industries. The decrease in productivity growth in no way bolsters the case for an industrial policy.

A CLOSER LOOK AT THE JAPANESE SUCCESS

The postwar flourishing of Japan's economy is frequently cited as the premier example of how successful an industrial policy can be. The Japanese do have a way of working cooperatively towards national economic objectives without getting strangled in bureaucratic red tape or dulling competition among business firms. But the contributions of MITI and of industrial policy to Japan's postwar success have been far overstated. Other factors were primarily responsible for the phenomenal growth that the Japanese economy enjoyed until very recently.

First, over the past two decades, the Japanese saved and invested some 30 to 35 percent of their GNP, compared to 17 to 20 percent in the United States.[8] Second, with an industrial plant technologically far behind those of the United States and Western Europe, Japanese business firms were able to put the huge savings to work at moderate risk and with good returns by upgrading their capital stock with known technologies. Countries that were much nearer to the technological frontier, like the United States, had to depend more heavily for their economic growth on the gradual advance of technical knowledge. Third, the Japanese appear to have developed a unique set of cooperative labor-management relationships that promote high quality work and rapid productivity growth.

Throughout the postwar period, the Japanese government in general, and MITI in specific, did act on a broad view of what was required for rapid economic growth in the particular cicumstances facing Japan. For example, private savings and investment were encouraged by tax laws and other measures. Up through the early 1970s, macroeconomic policies were highly expansive, but with a combination of very stimulative monetary policies and large budget surpluses. Thus, the government endeavored to encourage the rapid expansion of both demand and supply. Since it needed to import virtually all of its fuel and raw materials, Japan discouraged the import of manufactured goods. Especially in the earlier part of postwar history, when it was still lagging behind other major countries in industrial technology, Japan protected large segments of its home market against import competition.

But while a broad strategy along these lines did guide Japanese economic policy during the postwar period, that strategy did not dictate the detailed structure of Japanese industry. The major decisions about where funds would be invested were made by Japanese business leaders, not by MITI. Hugh Patrick, professor of Far Eastern economics at Yale has put forward this assessment:

> Indeed, looking at Japanese industrial development as a whole in the postwar period, I think the predominant source of its success was the entrepreneurial vigor of private enterprises that invested a good deal and took a lot of risks. The main role of the government was to provide an accommodating and supportive environment for the market, rather than providing leadership and direction. Unquestionably government planning bodies were important in a few industrial sectors, but not in many others which flourished on their own.[9]

The Japanese government, through its Fiscal Investment and Loan Program (FILP), does control substantial investment funds, amounting in 1980 to some $80 billion in direct investments, subsidized loans, and loan guarantees. Such a large investment budget does seem to offer potential leverage for carrying out an industrial policy. In fact, however, as Brookings' Philip Trezise carefully documented in the Spring, 1983 issue of the REVIEW, the government's investment portfolio is spread across a wide range of enterprises in response to regional, political, and special interest pressures. In 1979, the FILP budget was allocated among some fifty separate agencies, plus a number of local governments. The local governments, together with four agencies (a housing loan corporation, two small business financing entities, and the Japanese National Railways), got a total of 60 percent of the funds. Another 27 percent went to such entities as the Ex-Im Bank; the Japan Highway Corporation; the Japan Housing Corporation; the Agriculture, Forestry, and Fisheries Corporation; and the Japan Development Bank.

The Japan Development Bank (JDB), in turn, seems a likely candidate for the role of financing an industrial policy aimed at building up major growth industries. The facts belie this conjecture too. In the first twenty years of the JDB's life, according to Trezise, three quarters of its funds went to merchant shipping, electric utilities, and regional and urban development. The burgeoning steel industry, on the other hand, received during these two decades less than one percent ($110 million) of the JDB's financing. Since 1972, in Japan as in the United States, public investment has emphasized energy and pollution control—and the JDB budget reflects this trend. But JDB investment in the development of new technologies outside of the energy industry has averaged only $313 million a year over the last decade.

Thus, in Japan as in any other democratic country, the public investment budget has been divvied up in response to diverse political pressures. It has not been a major instrument for concentrating investment resources in carefully selected growth industries. Indeed, if one changed the institutional labels, the Japanese government's investment budget looks remarkably like what might have emerged from a House and Senate conference committee on public works in the United States Congress.

All of this is not to suggest that MITI had no influence on the direction of Japanese industrial investment. For example, MITI is widely, and probably quite correctly, cited as having played a major role in organizing the very successful Japanese penetration of the memory chip segment of the world semiconductor markets. As Paul Krugman has pointed out, however, the relevant question is whether this particular use of Japanese savings generated a higher return for the nation than would have been earned had the market allocated the funds. It may have done so, but we do not yet know the answer.

MITI has also had some major failures. For instance, MITI tried very hard—and, as is evident, to no avail—to keep Honda out of the automobile business and to consolidate Japanese auto production into a few giant companies. MITI also attempted to get a major commercial aircraft industry going in Japan, but the banks failed to follow MITI's lead and would not provide the necessary capital. Those who attribute Japan's economic success principally to MITI's industrial policy seem to be suggesting that without MITI the huge 30 to 35 percent of GNP that the Japanese invested in the past several decades would have gone mainly into such industries as textiles, shoes, plastic souvenirs, and fisheries. This is sheer nonsense. Given the quality of Japanese business executives, those massive investment funds probably would have wound up roughly where they actually did. And to the extent that there would have been differences, there is no reason to believe that MITI's influence, on balance, improved the choices in any major way.

The combination that worked so well for Japan—a huge saving rate, aggressive business leaders, and a backlog of modern technology waiting to be exploited—may now be faltering. In particular, as Japan has caught up to the technological frontier of other Western countries, the potential for large returns from investment in known technologies has been reduced. The propensity to save remains high, but investment opportunities appear to have dwindled. Partly for this reason, Japanese economic growth, while still above that in other advanced countries, fell from an average of 9.9 percent a year between 1960 and 1973 to 3.5 percent a year between 1973 and 1983.[11]

IDENTIFYING THE "RIGHT" INDUSTRIAL STRUCTURE

Despite the lack of evidence that the United States has been de-industrializing or that the key to Japan's economic success has been its industrial policy, advocates of an industrial policy for the United States nevertheless propose that the federal government play a much enlarged role in determining the structure of American industry. The centerpiece of an industrial policy is some kind of a development bank--a new Reconstruction Finance Corporation--with authority to do some or all of the following: provide loans, loan guarantees, and subsidies to business firms and regional development bodies; certify firms as being eligible for special tax breaks; recommend measures to protect domestic industries against competition from imports; and negotiate restructuring agreements with labor and management in firms and industries that are in trouble and are candidates for assistance. In major versions of industrial policy, the new RFC would be governed, or at least be advised, by a tripartite body made up of representatives from business, labor, and government. The powers of the Corporation would be exercised in pursuit of explicit industrial objectives designed to achieve some combination of the two broad goals--stimulating the emergence and growth of new high-tech industries and protecting and rehabilitating older industries.

The first problem for the government in carrying out an industrial policy is that we actually know precious little about identifying, before the fact, a "winning" industrial structure. There does not exist a set of economic criteria that determine what gives different countries preeminence in particular lines of business. Nor is it at all clear what the substantive criteria would be for deciding which older industries to protect or restructure.

Originally, comparative advantage and international specialization among countries were thought to derive principally from the relative abundance or scarcity of the factors of production--labor, capital, and various natural resources. The United States and other advanced industrial countries do in fact have a broad advantage in the production of those goods that are research-based and technologically sophisticated, and that require for their production an educated labor force. It is also demonstrably the case that the availability of certain kinds of natural resources can play an important role in determining comparative advantage. But beyond these very broad principles, there are no general criteria that allow one to predict the industries in which a country will be particularly successful.

Advanced industrial countries both export and import a wide range of goods that covers almost the entire spectrum of their manufacturing industries. Exports are not concentrated in one set of selected industries and imports in another. One study has shown, for example, that in major countries very few industries, classified at a medium (three digit) level of detail, had less than 30 percent of their international trade as intra-industry trade--i.e., in most categories of industrial goods, international trade involved significant volumes of both exports and imports, rather than exclusively one or the other. The distribution among advanced nations of the production of various manufactured products is not principally a function of some broad set of national characteristics, but arises in large part from quite different causes.

In an insightful article on industrial policy, Assar Lindbeck of the University of Stockholm has analyzed the origins of industrial specialization among advanced countries. He argues that what a country will specialize in is determined by a combination of historical coincidence and momentum. Individual entrepeneurs search for a niche in the market. Once one or more firms in a country successfully establish a foothold in the market for some special product, forces come into play that can heighten, at least for a while, that country's comparative advantage in the manufacture of that product. A growing market leads to economies of scale for the original producers. Ancillary firms spring up to supply the new industry's special needs. Workers and managers acquire skills and know-how. Success tends to breed success.

In short, the winners emerge from a very individualistic search process, only loosely governed by broad national advantages in relative labor, capital, or natural resource costs. The competence, knowledge, and specific attributes that go with successful entrepeneurship and export capability are so narrowly defined and so fine-grained that they cannot be assigned to any particular nation. The "winners" come from a highly decentralized search process, the results of which cannot be identified on the basis of abstract criteria. As Lindbeck pointed out, there is nothing in Swedish natural resources or national character that would have foreordained that Sweden would be preeminent in the production of ball bearings, safety matches, cream separators, and automatic lighthouses. Nor, it might be added, is there a basis in observable national characteristics to have predicted Japanese dominance in the motorcycle industry or the American success in pharmaceuticals and the export of construction management and design.

There are, of course, overall policies that government can pursue to create the kind of environment in which a decentralized search process is most likely to be fruitful. What government cannot do--except perhaps in a country that is far behind the leaders and simply trying to catch up by imitating them--is to identify in advance the particular lines and products in which its country will be successful.

Some have argued that a new industrial policy should particularly seek to reallocate investment towards industries with high value-added per worker and away from those with low value-added. The argument for such a reallocation implicitly assumes (1) that there are large numbers of skilled American workers trapped in low-paying jobs in industries with low value-added per worker; (2) that there are large untapped markets for the products of high value-added industries employing skilled workers; and (3) that this situation exists because of a propensity on the part of American business to invest too much in the low value-added, and too little in the high value-added industries. Government policies designed to improve the skills of the labor force make good sense. But given the current mix of skills in the labor pool, there is no evidence that market forces in the United States have tended to ignore potentially large returns in industries with high value-added per worker and to channel excessive investment to those with low value-added. Indeed, as Krugman points out, government redistribution of a fixed aggregate investment from low value-added to high value-added industries would tend to lower employment and output, since capital-labor and capital-output ratios are higher in the latter industries.

There are equally formidable barriers to designing substantively defensible criteria to govern a systematic government policy of trade protection and investment assistance for declining older industries. No one seriously suggests a policy of indiscriminate aid to all such industries, so some criteria for choice are necessary. One litmus test that is proposed is the importance of an industry to the national defense; that, however, is almost always a red herring. The national defense/essential industry argument is usually presented in an all-or-nothing mode, as though, in the absence of import protection, the affected industry would disappear. In fact, what is almost always at stake is a much less dramatic change in the industry's fortunes, of a magnitude that is irrelevant to national defense. Whether, for example, the domestic steel industry meets 80 percent of the nation's peacetime needs, as it does now, or only 60 percent is of no significance to the nation's security.

It has also been suggested that we assist those particular older and troubled industries that other governments are heavily subsidizing. The industries we would end up supporting under this decision rule would most likely be those with worldwide excess capacity, in which the returns to investment are unusually low, since those are the ones most apt to be getting help from other governments. A systematic reallocation of investment away from other American industries towards these would lower the growth of national output and real wages.

Ironically, the systematic provision of import protection to various industries, in an effort to "restructure" them, would indirectly weaken the most dynamic and progressive sector of American industry. Import protection would initially worsen the trade balances of the countries against whom it was directed. As a result, their currencies would tend to depreciate against the dollar. In turn, this would impair the competitive position of American export industries, which, by their very nature, are likely to be at the leading edge of economic progress. We would trade jobs and output in the leading sectors for jobs and output in the losing sectors.

In practice, the motivation behind most existing efforts to protect the losers is not so much to improve economic performance as to lessen the pains of economic change. Almost by definition, a dynamic economy is one in which change is continually at work—change in technology, in tastes, and in world markets. And while change creates new opportunities, it also forces some firms, workers, and communities to make painful adjustments.

A decent concern for the human costs imposed by economic change is one hallmark of a compassionate society. But society can act to reduce those costs in two quite different ways. First, it can short-circuit market forces and try to slow the pace of change through subsidies, trade protection, and regulations designed to prop up declining firms. Second, it can attempt to accommodate and ease the transitions dictated by changing economic conditions through the provision of reasonable unemployment compensation, relocation assistance, and generous training opportunities to those facing major adjustment problems. Neither approach will fully insulate workers and communities from the pains of economic change. But systematic application of the first approach, while preventing some pain for some people, will over time sap the economy of dynamism and hold down growth in living standards. The second option is far from perfect, but it offers the potential of reducing transition costs with much less impairment of the dynamism that generates economic growth.

INDUSTRIAL POLICY AND THE AMERICAN POLITICAL SYSTEM

Not only would it be impossible for the government to pick a winning industrial combination in advance, but its attempt to do so would almost surely inflict much harm.

There are many important tasks that only governments can do—and, with constant effort and watchfulness, they can do those tasks passably well. But the one thing that most democratic political systems—and especially the American one—cannot do well at all is to make critical choices among particular firms, municipalities, or regions, determining cold-bloodedly which shall prosper and which shall not. Yet such choices are precisely the kind that would have to be made—and made explicitly—for an industrial policy to become more than a political pork barrel.

The government can, and continually does, adopt policies that have the indirect consequence of harming particular individuals or groups. But a cardinal principle of American government is "never be seen to do direct harm." The formal and informal institutions of the political system are designed to hinder government from making hard choices among specific individuals, rewarding some and penalizing others. So it is, for example, that we have an Economic Development Administration, created to help "depressed areas", that has eligibility criteria so broad that they encompass over 80 percent of the counties in the United States. The same pattern—that of obviating the necessity of choice—is evident in the evoluton of the Model Cities Program. Two decades ago, planners in the Johnson administration set out to test the proposition that a very comprehensive assistance program—directed at physical capital, education, retraining, social services, and so on—that concentrated large investment in a few areas could overcome the inertial force and vicious cycle of inner city policy and decay. A demonstration of this approach was initially designed to be carried out in a very limited number of cities; hence the name "Model Cities Program." By the time the concept had made its way through the political thickets of the administration and the Congress, the Model Cities Program encompassed one hundred and fifty cities, each receiving only a fraction of the funding needed.

It is not surprising that the American political system is seldom capable of making express choices among individuals, firms, or regions. The American government, after all, was not established to bring order and authority out of social chaos. Quite to the contrary, it originated in an effort to reduce what was seen as too much authority on the part of the British king and parliament. Its founders were principally concerned to constrain legislative and executive authorities so that they could not make arbitrary and invidious choices among individuals. In the American system, most decisions that discriminate among specific citizens and firms are reached through litigation in the courts, where "fairness", rather than "efficiency", is the major criterion for settling disputes. When it is necessary to permit executive officials to make such decisions, their exercise of discretion is hedged about by complex procedural safeguards, including the right of appeal to the courts. The Administrative Procedures Act, which governs the exercise of regulatory authority, is a prime example of this approach.

The governmental choices that an industrial policy contemplates have little to do with fairness and much to do, at least ostensibly, with exacting economic criteria. As we have seen, these are precisely the sorts of decisions that the American political system makes very poorly. A new RFC would do not better. For every twenty new entrants into the high-tech race, nineteen will probably perish and only one succeed. But the federal government's portfolio would likely carry all twenty forever.

To be anything more than a universal protector of inefficiency, a systematic program of assistance to declining industries would have to call for some very hard-headed decisions among particular firms, cities, and groups of workers—that the Youngstown plant can live but the Weirton one must close, for example, or that the cotton textile industry has a reasonable chance to rehabilitate itself but the wool textile industry is a hopeless case and must die. Or that in order for the steel industry to compete successfully in world markets, the large increases over the last fifteen years in its wages and fringe benefits relative to those of the rest of industry must be eliminated. Quite apart from the inability of any staff to make such substantive calls correctly, can anyone imagine an American RFC being left alone to make such decisions, with its authorizations and appropriations controlled by the Congress and its policies supervised by a president interested in his own and his party's political success? Rather, we can expect a combination of patterns to emerge: Some assistance would be made available, on a formula basis, to all industries that were in trouble; the wheels with the loudest squeaks might get a bit of extra financial grease; and protectionist interests would have a new and highly vulnerable pressure point to exploit. In the process, resources would be misallocated, incentives for industrial efficiency reduced, and competitive forces blunted.

THE FALSE ALLURE OF "COORDINATION"

One of the most frequently heard arguments for industrial policy is that it would bring a much-needed coordination to government policy-making. Those who make this argument begin by pointing out that the government already has in place many individual policies that affect the industrial structure, often in illogical, contradictory, or harmful ways. They go on to ask why we do not, therefore, adopt a positive and coherent industrial policy in place of the current ad hoc array. These advocates often cite examples of the foolishness that ad hoc assistance decisions lead to:

o The U.S. government now spends five times more on research and development for commercial fishing than for steel.

o The U.S. tax code provides almost $750 million a year in tax breaks for the timber industry, but only a small fraction of that amount for semiconductors.

o We now provide substantial import protection for the carbon and specialty steel industries (an illustration presumably adduced on the grounds that with an industrial policy we would be able to extract more competition-oriented reforms from labor and management in the favored industries).

In fact, this argument makes little sense--even if the examples cited are indeed blunders. It might very well be bad policy to spend five times more on R&D for commercial fishing than for steel (although what is relevant is total R&D, private as well as government, and even then it is not self-evident that the payoff from R&D in commercial fishing is less than from R&D in steel). Tax experts long ago concluded that the special treatment of the timber industry was excessively generous. And virtuallly all economists would argue that the steel protectionist measures are bad for the country. But these conclusions would all be true even if the term "industrial policy" had never been invented, and regardless of whether industrial production was an increasing or decreasing share of GNP. Indeed, it is curious logic to cite examples of how the American industrial structure has been distorted by political pressures--in support of an argument for entrusting even more economic decisions to the same political system. One does not have to be a cynic to forecast that the surest way to multiply unwarranted subsidies and protectionist measures is to legitimize their existence under the rubric of industrial policy. The likely outcome of an industrial policy that encompassed some elements of both "protecting the losers" and "picking the winners" is that the losers would back subsidies for the winners in return for the latter's support on issues of trade protection.[14]

The argument is also made that we do provide assistance to individual firms, on occasion and in a very ad hoc way; the Chrysler and Lockheed bailouts are usually cited as examples. Should we not, therefore, regularize and rationalize this procedure, rather than making these assistance decisions on a case-by-case basis? In fact, the ad hoc approach is precisely the right approach. To every rule there are exceptions. It may very occasionally be in the public interest to supercede the market's judgment and to prevent the bankruptcy of some major firm. But it is a virtue that a special law is now needed for each case. It is a virtue that each case is, in fact, treated as an exception. Only very exceptional cases are likely to muster the support needed to enact a special law, and the government's bargaining power, to impose needed and painful reforms on management and labor, is consequently enhanced. Should this process of decision by exception be supplanted by an ongoing authority to initiate bailouts, the result would almost surely be a politically vulnerable fund, available to help avoid or delay politically sensitive plant closings.

SOME REAL PROBLEMS

To say that industrial policy is a dangerous solution for an imaginary problem is not to say that the United States has no serious economic difficulties. It has a number of them.

Our most immediate set of problems is macroeconomic in nature. Recovery from the deepest recession of the postwar period has just begun. Having paid a very high price for partially wringing out a stubborn inflation fifteen years in the making, we—along with every other industrial country—will have to walk a very fine line to sustain an economic recovery vigorous enough to make substantial inroads on unemployment, but not so buoyant as to risk a resurgence of inflationary pressures or inflationary expectations.

In addition, we in the United States face the special problem of a political impasse that threatens to perpetuate very sizeable federal budget deficits even as the economy recovers toward full utilization of its resources. Since the Federal Reserve is most unlikely to accommodate these high employment deficits with large and inflationary increases in the money supply, failure to break the impasse with tax increases and spending cuts would extend today's high real interest rates—or, more likely, even higher ones —into the indefinite future. This outcome would have particularly serious consequences for the health of America's industrial structure. High interest rates would tend to perpetuate overvaluation of the U.S. dollar, and would continue to penalize American exports and encourage imports. At home, the high interest rates would especially depress purchases of durable manufactured goods. Finally, the ability of new and young enterprises, at the frontiers of technological advance, to raise new capital could be seriously impaired to the extent that the actuality and the expectation of continued high interest rates depressed stock market values.

Getting America's monetary and fiscal policies in order is far more important for the health of the nation's industrial structure than any conceivable set of new industrial policies. What now seems to be serious problems of industrial structure would quickly shrink and become far more manageable with a few years of balanced economic recovery at lower real interest rates.

After the achievement of a sustained and balanced recovery, the prospects for which depend heavily on how the government uses its macroeconomic tools, the next most important factors influencing industrial performance are mainly beyond the government's control--such things as the pace of technological progress, the course of labor-management relationships, and the stability of world markets. There is, however, a variety of governmental microeconomic policies that can affect, favorably or unfavorably, the vigor and adaptability of American industry. Choices among alternatives in this area sometimes pose very difficult tradeoffs between economic efficiency and other social goals. For example, environmental considerations compete with the objective of keeping industrial costs low. The provision of generous tax incentives for risk bearing has to be balanced with the objective of a more equal distribution of income. Additional federal support for scientific and technical education would conflict with the goal of budget expenditure control. In other cases, what is at issue is not a tradeoff among competing national objectives, but the reform or elimination of provisions in tax or regulatory codes that distort the pattern of investment among different industries. The 1981 liberalization of depreciation allowances, for example, was desirable in the aggregate but very arbitrary as among investments of different types. It sharply skewed rates of return and distorted investment incentives among industries. Determining the federal government's stance on these and other thorny issues will continue to provide grist for the legislative and political mills in the years ahead. How they are settled will have an important, if not overwhelming, influence on the behavior of American industries.

The most critical and vexing structural problems that American society will have to face in the coming decade have little to do with the issues raised by industrial policy. Even with a return to prosperity, unemployment among America's black youth will remain scandalously high. Large parts of American central cities will continue to be afflicted by serious financial constraints, social problems, and physical decay. And, if recent studies are to be believed, the quality of American education has been deteriorating for a number of years. Unfortunately, no one yet seems to have a very clear idea of exactly how the federal government can best play a constructive role in fundamentally reversing these very troubling structural trends. But we must keep searching for solutions—and where federal outlays are required to experiment with promising approaches, there are the areas, unlike most others, where the benefit of the doubt ought to be given a little more rather than a little less funding.

In sum, there are changes in federal fiscal and monetary policies that could help the economy generally, and industry in particular, attain a more satisfactory level of economic prosperity. There are microeconomic policies that we know could contribute to an environment that is favorable to the creation of new and rapidly expanding lines of business and to the adaptability of American industry. In many cases, formulating these policies requires making some very difficult choices among competing national objectives.

In addition, there are a few very important structural problems for which, at the moment, no convincing solutions are in sight. Yet it is absolutely essential that we keep searching and experimenting to try to solve them.

One structural problem, however, that does not exist is the de-industrialization of American industry. And one set of government measures that we do not need is an industrial policy under which the federal government tries to play an important role in determining the allocation of resources to individual firms and industries.

We have enough real problems without creating new ones.

NOTES

1. Ira Magaziner and Robert Reich, Minding America's Business, Harcourt Brace Jovanovich, New York, 1982, p. 4.

2. In a forthcoming Brookings book, Robert Z. Lawrence documents in substantial detail the absence of any trend toward de-industrialization in the United States during the 1970s and in particular, the fallacy of the proposition that international trade has contributed to depressing output and employment in American manufacturing. This section of the paper owes much to his work.

3. To reduce distortions caused by cyclical influences (U.S. recessions in 1970 and 1980), average output in 1969-1970 and 1979-1980 was used to make the decade output comparisons. The European average was held down by the very poor performance of the United

Kingdom, but even if the United Kingdom is excluded from these calculations, the growth of manufacturing output in the United States still exceeded that of the rest of Europe as reported by the OECD data. The U.S. Bureau of Labor Statistics produces an alternative set of manufacturing output measures for selected countries; according to these data, the United States outperformed Germany and the average of eight European countries, but grew less than the European average (33.5 versus 36 percent) if the United Kingdom is excluded.

4. During the cyclical peak of the Vietnam war boom, 1965-69, the constant-dollar manufacturing share averaged slightly higher (30 percent) than it did in both the early years of that decade (28.2 percent) and the last years of the 1970s (28.6 percent), but by no more than can be explained by the strength of the boom. In a regression equation fit to data from 1955-80 that linked the manufacturing share to a cyclical variable and a time trend, the time trend did have a very small negative coefficient of marginal statistical significance. The trend was so slight that it would require some thirty years to reduce the share by one percentage point. There was no evidence that the trend became larger in the 1970s.

5. Marc Bendick, Jr., and Ruth Radlinski, "Workers Dislocated by Economic Change: Do They Need Federal Employment?," National Commission for Employment Policy, Seventh Annual Report, Appendix B.

6. Long-term unemployment rates (percent of the labor force) in 1979 were: United States (1.14), United Kingdom (1.92), France (4.41), Germany (3.35). The long-term unemployment definition—fifteen weeks or longer for the U.S., fourteen weeks for the U.K., and three months for France and Germany—does bias the U.S. rate down relative to the others, but not enough to account for those differences. Economic Report of the President, January, 1981, p. 127. These findings were confirmed by a later OECD analysis reported in Economic Outlook, July, 1983, p. 46 (Table 15).

7. Martin Neil Baily estimated, more generally, that none of the slowdown in American productivity growth since 1973 can be explained by a shifting composition of output among major American industries. Baily, "The Productivity Growth Slowdown by Industry," Brookings Papers on Economic Activity, 2:1982, pp. 445-51.

8. Based on OECD estimates of gross fixed capital formation as a percent of gross domestic product (GDP). Economic Outlook 1960-1980, Table R-3. The difference between GDP and GNP is small and does not the affect basic comparison between the United States and Japan.

9. Interview in Manhattan Report on Economic Policy, Manhattan Institute for Policy Research, Vol. II, No. 7, October, 1982.

10. Paul Krugman, "Targeted Industrial Policies: Theory and Evidence," a paper prepared for the Conference on Industrial Change and Public Policy, sponsored by the Federal Reserve Bank of Kansas City, August 25-26, 1983, pp. 46-49.

11. 1983 growth as forecast by the OECD, Economic Outlook, July, 1983.

12. Assar Lindbeck, "Industrial Policy as an Issue in the Economic Environment," The World Economy, December 1981, pp. 391-405.

13. Krugman, op. cit., pp. 6-8.

14. The chief executive of a firm producing semiconductors has recently argued that his industry does not need special government help—only a "Buy America" provision for its products.

From the Brookings Review, Fall 1983. Copyright 1983 by the Brookings Institution, Washington, D.C.

NIP in the Air: Fashionable Myths of National Industrial Policy

Richard B. McKenzie

The debate over a national industrial policy has been framed in much political rhetoric that colorfully charts the demise of the United States as an industrial power in the world economy. Harvard University Professor Robert Reich proclaims in the opening page of his widely read book, "Since the late 1960's America's economy has been slowly unraveling."[1] Not only is industry in serious decline, but "America's politics have been in chronic disarray."[2]

After attributing the country's economic decline to the inability or unwillingness of business managers to discard production techniques developed during and reserved for an earlier economic epoch of standardized mass production, Professor Reich deduces that businesses must be coaxed into becoming more "adaptive" and inclined to adopt what he calls flexible-system production: "America has a choice: It can adapt itself to the new economic realities [advancing technologies, accelerating capital mobility, and growing world competitiveness] by altering its organization, or it can fail to adapt and thereby continue its present decline...But failure to adapt will rend the social fabric irreparable. Adaptation is America's challange. It is America's next frontier."[3]

Economists Barry Bluestone and Bennett Harrison document what they perceive to be "the Deindustrialization of America," arguing (as Professor Reich and others conclude) that the country's path to economic salvation lies not in less government, as the Reagan administration proposes, but in more government control of the economy, especially the investment sector.[4] Specifically, a growing chorus of advocates of a centralized and coordinated industrial policy stress that many of our economic ills can be resolved through instituting industrial democracy, an economic environment in which workers, managers, and government officials participate jointly (through discussions and voting power) at the firm level in investment and reinvestment decisions and at the national level in the allocation of the nation's capital stock across regions and industries.[5] In addition to beefing up federal expenditures on the nation's infrastructure and a wide range of social services--education, child care, health care--industrial policy proponents contend that the country must "rationalize" investment decisions through federal loans, interest subsidies, loan guarantees, and grants.

The purpose of these proposed new programs is to save firms from falling prey to international competitors, to spur the emergence of the so-called sunrise industries, and generally to ease transition problems faced by workers and communities in a changing industrial climate. After all, the proponents contend, we need a social organization premised on "equity, security, and participation," not "greed and fear."[6] Not surprisingly, the type of industrial policy advocated depends often on the private interests and concerns of the advocate. "The kind of industrial policy I'm talking about," writes Edward Jefferson of E.I. du Pont de Nemours & Company, "should be highly selective, limited to asserting the national interest on behalf of our declining industries. That's no different from the concern we expressed for agriculture when it was in great difficulty in this country."[7] Professor Reich would settle simply for making the federal government not larger, just "more open, more explicit, and more strategic."[8] Others in the industrial policy movement seek nothing short of centralized economic planning.[9]

After the rhetoric is stripped away, it becomes clear that many, if not most, industrial policy reformers seek a substantial realignment of public and private decision making in the country. These reforms are premised on the undeniable contention that several key industries—automobiles, steel, housing, and rubber—have recently experienced considerable economic difficulty. However, the reforms are also predicated upon a modern industrial mythology. And before serious reform can be considered, six key myths need to be dispelled.

MYTH 1

THE MANUFACTURING SECTOR IN THE UNITED STATES IS ON THE WANE, RAPIDLY GIVING RISE TO A SHIFT IN EMPLOYMENT OPPORTUNITIES FROM HIGH-PAYING INDUSTRIAL JOBS TO LOW-PAYING SERVICE JOBS.

Professor Lester Thurow of the Massachusetts Institute of Technology began his congressional testimony on industrial policy pressing the widely held view that "interest in industrial policy springs from a simple four-letter word—fear. American industry is being beaten up by its international competition, and business and labor are both afraid that American industry is going down for the count."[10] Similarly, the U.S. Trade Policy Council argues, "American jobs and markets are being systematically eroded, eaten away by a few of our trading partners who do not practice the same kind of free and fair trade that we do."[11] After calculating the jobs lost to private disinvestment during the 1970s, Bluestone and Harrison conclude, "What people seem to be feeling (and what most analysts in universities and in the media seem to be studiously misunderstanding) is a deepening sense of insecurity, growing out of the collapse all around them of the traditional economic base of their communities. Their very jobs are being pulled out from under them. And instead of providing new employment opportunities, a higher standard of living, and enhanced security, the decisions of corporate managers are doing just the opposite."[12]

But have manufacturing employment and production, not to mention total employment and gross national product, been in serious decline in the United States? The data clearly dispel any lingering impression that the nation's total stock of jobs is regressing. Admittedly, the unemployment rate rose gradually during the 1960s and 1970s, reaching a peak of 10.8 percent in December 1982, the depth of the 1980-1983 recessionary period. The growth in the unemployment rate was due in part to the purposeful (but clumsy) anti-inflationary policy of the Federal Reserve from 1979 to 1982 and to an increase in the labor participation rate, especially by women, which in turn was due partly to the rising tax burden and desire of many families to maintain their standard of living through two incomes. However, total nonagriculture employment rose by 30 million, or by almost 50 percent, between 1965 (60.6 million) and 1980 (90.8 million); by 29 percent between 1970 (70.6 million) and 1980; and by 19 percent between 1975 (76.8 million) and 1980. In the fifteen years prior to 1965, nonagriculture employment expanded by much less, by a little more than 35 percent.

Such a comparison of employment growth between the 1950-1965 and 1965-1980 periods fails to support the widely held view that the economy is, on balance, systematically destroying jobs. Yes, jobs are constantly being destroyed as new ones are being created in private markets. But the history of progress is necessarily a history of job destruction. Many of the jobs created by the expanding industries destroy the jobs of contracting industries as workers freely seek better opportunities.

Although there have been obvious ups and downs, the trend in manufacturing employment for the country as a whole remained largely flat from 1965 to 1980, moving between 18.5 million and 21 million workers and increasing a scant compound rate of 0.4 percent over the 1965 to 1980 period. Proponents of industrial policy often stress the million or so manufacturing jobs lost between 1969 and 1975, failing to recognize the rather dramatic growth in manufacturing employment of approximately 3 million jobs between 1975 and 1979.

Those are the facts of employment. The clamor for an industrial policy, then, appears to boil down to four central concerns. First, the 1981-1982 recession took a serious toll on manufacturing employment, as well as total employment. Manufacturing employment fell by nearly 4 million jobs, or by 20 percent, between 1979 and December 1982. But that decline, due mainly to deliberate anti-inflationary policies pursued erratically by the Federal Reserve, was largely cyclical, not structural. Although there are ongoing structural shifts in employment in the economy, this is not one of them. Perhaps the advocates of a national industrial policy are too afflicted with tunnel vision to have noticed the revival of manufacturing employment that is accompanying the recovery.

Second, several key industries—specifically automobiles, steel, rubber, textiles, and related products—were in serious decline during the 1970s, especially the late 1970s. Even the decline in the basic industries was not as dramatic as has been supposed. Between 1970 and 1980, employment in the motor vehicle and equipment industries fell from 799,000 to 789,000, or by only 1.3 percent. Employment in primary metals industries during the same period fell by 118,000, which was only 9 percent of the 1970 labor force. (Employment in fabricated metal products actually rose slightly during the 1970s.) Again, these industries have recently suffered heavy employment losses, which were at least partially a cyclical problem. Moreover, this was a period of expansion for other industries, including computers, biogenetics, robotics, and other high-tech products.

Third, between 1965 and 1980, manufacturing employment tended to shift among regions. As a consequence, the flatness in manufacturing employment for the entire country is not observed in all Census Bureau divisions. There was a general DECLINE in employment in the Northeast and a general expansion in the West and South. The trend for the North Central division was flat. The contraction in Northeast manufacturing employment over the fifteen-year period, however, hides a strong turnaround in manufacturing employment between 1976 and 1980. In those four years New England experienced a compound rate of annual manufacturing employment expansion of 3.46 percent, earning the nickname "Sunbelt of the North." North Central manufacturing employment, meanwhile, expanded at a compound rate of less than 1 percent. The growth in manufacturing employment in the West and South was substantially higher than in the Northeast and the North Central. The important point is that from 1965 to 1980, total employment in all regions—indeed, all states—expanded, although irregularly and slowly at times.

Fourth, manufacturing employment has declined in a relative sense. In 1965 manufacturing employment counted for approximately 30 percent of all nonagriculture jobs. By 1980 the share of the country's jobs in manufacturing was down to 22 percent, still on par with the share of jobs in manufacturing in 1947. The growth of jobs from 1965 to 1980 was most apparent in the government and service sectors. Contrary to what is often suggested—that the shift from manufacturing to service jobs means workers are becoming janitors and fast-food waiters—these shifts in the composition of the labor force have economic explanations.

Many of the service jobs have been taken by women, teenagers, and elderly people who seek part-time employment demanding few skills. Such jobs satisfy a need.

The service sector includes more than janitorial and waitering services. Of the 9 million service jobs created during the 1970s, which caused a 41 percent increase in service employment between 1970 and 1980, 1 million (representing a 68 percent increase) were in business services, and another 6.7 million (a 54 percent increase) were in professional services, a category that covers health, education, welfare, and religious employment. Employment in finance, insurance, and real estate expanded from 3.9 million in 1970 to 6 million in 1980 (a 52 percent expansion). Personal services actually contracted by 10 percent during the decade.

A significant portion of the shift occurred not because manufacturing plants were replaced by fast-food parlors in which workers had to accept employment, but because many manufacturers could not meet the rising wages of their competitors in the service (and expanding manufacturing) industries and could not, therefore, hold their employees. In short, the rise in service employment was often the result of free choices of U.S. workers seeking improvement in their welfare. The idea that firms are always responsible for jobs destroyed is a gross distortion of the way employment markets work.

The contraction of employment in many key manufacturing industries in the 1970s was partly a response to productivity improvements that resulted in a steady rise in the real value of manufactured goods over the past two decades, from $171.8 billion in 1960 to $351.2 billion in 1980. What seems to be bothering advocates of an industrial policy is that the increases in output were not always accompanied by increases in wages. Indeed, average gross weekly wages stayed more or less the same during most of the 1970s and have declined every year since 1970, facts that can be explained by the growing competitiveness of many industries. Just as manufacturing workers have benefited in the past from productivity increases in agriculture and computers, other workers through their purchases are benefiting from productivity improvements in key manufacturing industries.

Some of the contraction in manufacturing employment and wages experienced during the late 1970s was due to workers' uncompetitive wage demands. Steelworkers, for example, were able to negotiate wage increases even when their productivity was declining. In other words, not all job losses can be attributed to poor management decisions (which also, of course, play a role in labor force losses), and many of the job losses were caused by those who risked unemployment by raising wages to uncompetitive levels.

Lester Thurow, among others, blames imports for the stagnating or declining positions of a number of basic industries. But consider the assessment of Professors Joseph Badaracco and David Yoffie, who write, "Fortunately for America and unfortunately for proponents of industrial policy, a crisis of catastrophic proportions is not yet upon us. The deterioration in the United States' international position is real, but it is not as widespread or calamitous as many believe."[13]

Professors Badaracco and Yoffie question the view that the country's failures in international markets are culturally inspired—that is, reflective of U.S. executives' inablility or unwillingness to adapt. Although the Unitd States had an overall trade deficit in 1981, it also had trade surpluses in capital goods, agriculture, and industrial supplies. The U.S. surplus in high-technology goods, for example, is growing, as is the nation's share of trade in manufactured goods since 1978. This rise in world market share has occurred despite lagging productivity increases and decreases in the international value of the dollar, caused in part by relatively high real interest rates in the United States, which have attracted foreign investment. And that, in turn, has fortified domestic demand for capital goods.

Finally, it is a gross distortion of the facts and benefits of international trade for proponents of industrial policies to develop their case by pointing to the U.S. trade deficits with Japan and other important trading partners without acknowledging our trade surpluses with other countries (specifically, European coun-) tries or recognizing that Japan has trade deficits with other countries that use the dollars obtained from Japan to finance their deficits with the United States. U.S. trade deficits with Japan are financed, in part, by U.S. trade surpluses with other countries that have trade deficits with Japan. Moreover, a contraction of the U.S. trade deficit with Japan will lead to a contraction of the U.S. trade surplus with other countries. Our problems cannot be tackled simply by restricting our trade deficit with a particular country.

MYTH 2 (a Corollary to Myth 1)

THE COUNTRY'S EMPLOYMENT BASE IS RAPIDLY CHANGING. HIGHPAYING MANUFACTURING JOBS ARE BEING REPLACED BY LOW-PAYING SERVICE JOBS. THE RAPIDITY OF THESE CHANGES IS SO GREAT THAT DRAMATIC NEW GOVERNMENT INITIATIVES ARE NEEDED TO EASE THE PAIN OF ADJUSTMENT.

Most Democratic candidates for president have premised their industrial policy proposals on what they perceive are substantial changes in the composition of jobs. Sen. Gary Hart echoes a familiar theme, "Over the last 30 years, the U.S. economy has been undergoing a transformation as significant as the Industrial Revolution of the 19th century."[14] Rep. John LaFalce in opening hearings on industrial policy before the House Subcommittee on Economic Stabilization noted, "We are witnessing an unprecedented period of change in our economic life, with an increasingly internationalized economy, declining basic industry, high unemployment, and staggering rates of change in knowledge and technology."[15]

The myth that the country is rapidly being transformed from an economy emphasizing housing, automobiles, and steel to computers and telecommunications is believed by two-thirds of the respondents to a national survey. Columnist Robert Samuelson has noted, "These perceptions are to history as bourbon is to water."[16] Many of the facts presented above in discussing the myth of industrial decay should disabuse people of their misperceptions. How could we be going through a period of industrial change of staggering proportions when, as advocates of industrial policy point out, we are experiencing, by historical standards, relatively low and at times non-existent increases in productivity? Granted, changes have been observed, but the evidence suggests that if the private sector has been able to advance and cope with much more rapid rates of technological change in the past, it should certainly be able to handle the current changes.

The persistence of the myth can be explained by the attention the media give to developments in computer technology (which many people find mysterious), the closing of plants in key industries, and the recent relatively high unemployment rates. Furthermore, statistics on projected job growth can be used artfully to suit the purposes of the industrial policy advocate. If, as Mr. Samuelson observes, the interest of the "policy peddler" (his term) is to stress the rapid emergence of high-tech jobs, he can focus on the percentage growth projected by the Labor Department for several key high-tech industries in the 1979-1990 period: paralegal personnel (109 percent), data-processing mechanics (92 percent), computer operators (72 percent), and computer analysts (68 percent).

Alternatively, if the industrial policy advocate wants to convince the audience that the nation is being transformed into a country of relatively low skilled workers, he can emphasize the absolute number of jobs expected to emerge over the 1980s in selected job categories: secretaries (700,000), nurses' aides and orderlies (508,000), janitors (501,000), and sales clerks (479,000), most of whom receive below-average wages. These analyses, however, are gross distortions because they do not consider the number of workers already in the various job categories. As Mr. Samuelson writes, "If there are already a lot of janitors (and there are), a big job increase may mean that the janitorial work force is just keeping pace with the economy's expansion. In fact, this is precisely what is expected to happen. In 1980, there were 2.8 million janitors and 2.9 million sales clerks. Projected growth for these occupations parallels total growth."[17]

The Labor Department[18] does not forecast dramatic changes in the composition of the labor force between now and 1990. Education, agriculture, and private household services are expected to be the only major sectors of the economy that will experience declines in employment over the period, and those sectors are not of special concern to industrial policy advocates.[19] Although declines in particular job categories and industries are expected, total manufacturing employment will continue to grow very slowly, even with the more conservative assumptions about overall growth in the economy.[20] The percentage of the nation's labor force in manufacturing will continue to decline as other sectors expand more rapidly, but although the precise projection may be off the mark, manufacturing employment growth is expected. Manufacturing jobs, on balance, are not expected to be wiped out, as many industrial policy advocates imply.

Industries are not expected to grow at the same rates; employment in a number of sectors is expected to decline. Employment in most industries is expected to change at average annual rates of 3.1 percent to -1.5 percent. Such rates do not support the view that the economy will be dramatically restructured by 1990. Admittedly, the impact of relatively small annual changes can mount over the course of a decade. However, the industries that will be expanding rapidly in the 1980s were relatively small at the start of the decade; relatively large growth in an industry like computers will, as a consequence, do little to change the composition of the nation's employment by 1990.

MYTH 3

THE FEDERAL GOVERNMENT SAVED CHRYSLER FROM BANKRUPTCY.

The federal government's aid to the Chrysler Corporation in 1979 is touted as the quintessential example of what industrial policy, strategically aimed at helping firms out of financial crisis, can accomplish. Former Vice President Walter Mondale, now a Democratic contender for the presidency, exhorted union leaders,

> Look at Chrysler. I believe in a free market. Most decisions have to be made there. But there are times when things are so important that that's why we have a government of the United States. If we had let Chrysler go down the drain, we would have lost a major competitor in the auto industry. We would have lost a major source of industrial productivity in our country. The federal government would have lost billions of dollars through the cost of unemployment and the collapse of the industry and the tax losses and all that went with it.... Many people, including the man who is now President, turned his back on Chrysler and said, "No help."
>
> I'm proud of the fact that I worked for the auto workers and the auto industry to drive a quality recommendation through our administration to support that Chrysler loan and help pass it in Congress. Three years later, the Chrysler Corporation is one of the success stories in America. It's starting to make progress. It's paying the federal government back. We're making money off the loan. The communities with plants are stabilizing. People have jobs. We've got more competition in the auto industry. What's wrong with using the government when it serves?[21]

If one judges the bailout in terms of whether Chrysler still exists, then the bailout worked. But Chrysler might have survived even if bankruptcy proceedings had begun in 1979. Indeed, attorney James Hickle declares that for all practical purposes "the Chrysler Corporation has gone bankrupt. Or, more accurately, in the past three years Chrysler has renegotiated its debt and restructured its organization in a way that greatly resembles a company that has gone through bankruptcy."[22]

Mr. Hickle points out that the bailout law required Chrysler's creditors to make "concessions," a provision that was pressed by then Secretary of the Treasury G. William Miller and enabled Chrysler to pay off more than $600 million in loans at 30 cents on the dollar and to convert $700 million in loans into a special class of preferred stock, a class of stock that according to Mr. Hickle is "relatively worthless in the financial markets, because the shares presently earn no dividends and are unredeemable for several years. Granted, these preferred stockholders were able to take their shares of preferred for common in early 1983; however, it is fair to believe that the market value of the newly acquired common stock will be less that the value of the original, plus lost interest."[23] Had the company been allowed to declare bankruptcy, the changes in Chrysler's balance sheet might have been a little different, except that stockholders and creditors would probably have taken a greater financial beating. But that is the risk of investing in private enterprise, and stockholders and lenders are compensated through dividends and interest rates.

Did the bailout save jobs? That is questionable for several reasons. First, the company could have started anew after bankruptcy proceedings, as many other companies do, and it could be employing as many workers as the "New Chrysler Corporation" currently does. Second, other investors (including any number of other companies) could have purchased Chrysler's assets at the postbankruptcy market price, and production could have continued, perhaps on a more modest but profitable scale. Third, other car companies could have emerged or expanded, providing jobs in the process. Fourth, lendable funds were drawn away from other firms and other investment purposes. Some Chrysler jobs were saved, but jobs in other firms were just as surely destroyed. And finally, since Chrysler has cut its white-collar work force by 20,000 and its production work force by 42,600, there is ample reason for Senator William Proxmire and others to wonder whether the bailout actually saved any jobs at all.[24] Certainly if the government treated all firms like Chrysler, as industrial policy advocates suggest it should, Chrysler's workers would find the benefits of the bailout more questionable. The employees, stockholders, suppliers, and customers of each bailed out company would have to carry the heavy tax burden of salvaging tens of thousands of other companies.

In addition, Mr. Hickel questions whether Chrysler is actually recovering. First, half of Chrysler's reported $170 million in profits comes from large losses that were carried forward to 1983 and beyond, reducing its tax liability. Second, the company cut its real expenditures on research and development by 18 percent, cutbacks that could hamper future profitability. Given its cutbacks in purchases of plant and equipment, Chrysler may be forsaking long-term profitability for short-run profits, something that has not gone unrecognized by industry analysts. Chrysler managed to defer $220 million in wage concessions for 1982 and 1983; some of that was given back under the threat of a strike in 1982, and more givebacks are expected to be negotiated in early 1984.[25] The company can also thank "voluntary restrictions" accepted on the importation of Japanese cars, which at this writing the Japanese are refusing to continue. Finally, any success Chrysler has in staying out of the red may be due more to the special entrepreneurial skills of chairman Lee Iaccoca than to the federal bailout.

In short, there is every reason to believe that Mr. Hickel was right when he wrote, "In reality, the primary difference between the actual bankruptcy that Chrysler faced in 1979 and the quasi-bankruptcy that Chrysler has gone through in the past three years, is that under this quasi-bankruptcy the federal government has accepted responsibility for guaranteeing over $1 billion in Chrysler loans. But if Chrysler's creditors and employees have already suffered through the debt negotiations and layoffs that typify reorganizations under the bankruptcy laws, who is benefiting from those loan guarantees? Primarily Chrysler's stockholders."[26]

MYTH 4

THE POSTWAR JAPANESE ECONOMIC MIRACLE HAS BEEN TO A SUBSTANTIAL DEGREE THE WORK OF THE JAPANESE GOVERNMENT.

Political scientist Chalmers Johnson contends that "central to understanding Japan's economic 'miracle'—the unprecedented economic growth—is the role of the Ministry of International Trade and Industry (MITI)."[27] Professor Lester Thurow concludes, "While the foreign success (in outcompeting the United States in international trade) is traceable to many factors (low currency values, more engineers, longer time horizons), it remains true that each of these countries that are now beating up on American industry has some mechanism for strategic coordination of their industries. In Japan the banking system is heavily influenced by the decisions of government, MITI tries to develop a consensus for its industrial policies, and 'administrative guidance' is a way of life."[28] Professor Robert Reich adds (referring to the industrial policies of several countries, including Japan),

> As relatively late industrializers, dependent on international trade, continental Europe and Japan relied to a far greater extent than did America or Britain on national economic strategies, spearheaded by their governments. In sharp contrast to the American pattern, these govern-

ments were the driving force behind economic development —the vehicles through which middle-class business interests overcame the inertia of an older economic order based on landed wealth...They were, in short, directly and openly intervening to propel their economies toward growth. In several of these countries—especially Japan, West Germany, and France—these public efforts have successfully accelerated economic adjustment.[29]

Although government policies certainly played a role in the economic development of Japan, claims of Japan's industrial policy successes are grossly exaggerated, given the limited role the Japanese government played in the economy, relative to the United States and other countries. During the 1950s, 1960s, and 1970s, only 10 to 15 percent of outstanding loans were financed through government institutions, and government-sponsored capital formation represented less that 10 percent of the country's gross national expenditures.[30] However, government involvement in capital formation expanded gradually over the last three decades, and that policy accompanied a slowdown in Japan's economic growth.

Granted, the Japanese government was responsible for 28 percent of research and development projects in 1980. But the government's share of R&D expenditures in the United States was 51 percent, and in West Germany, 44 percent. Furthermore, only 1.5 percentage points of the Japanese government's 28 percent R&D share went into private industrial R&D, whereas 25 percentage points of the United States' 51 percent share and 12.5 percentage points of West Germany's 44 percent share went for private industrial R&D.[31]

Japan's Fiscal Investment and Loan Program (FILP), which is independent of the government's budget and designed to invest in government and private enterprises, provides considerable government aid to selected industries that may permit Japan to "beat up" on U.S. industries. FILP's budget for 1980 was set at 18 trillion yen or more that $80 billion, which is spread among fifty separate entities and local governments.[32] Typically, the spread is 20 percent to local governments, 30 percent to public investment, and 50 percent to something called "policy implementation finanancing."[33]

Japan's policy-implementation funds seem directly related to industrial planning, although the local government and public investment expenditures can also have positive effects on infrastructure and, thereby, economic growth. The United States, however, has also been heavily involved in such expenditures at all levels of government. Since the inception of Japan's policy implementation program, approximately 75 to 80 percent of the funds (which, again, accounted for approximately 50 percent of the FILP budget) were lent to small businesses, homeowners, farmers, and "others" which included the Japan National Railway.[34] As Philip Trezise, senior fellow at the Brookings Institution, has observed, these borrowers "may provide many worthy services to Japanese society, but it is difficult to credit any of them with being closely connected with promising growth sectors, unless housing is so considered."[35]

The remaining 20 to 25 percent of the policy-implementation funds went mainly to the Japan Development Bank and the Export-Import Bank of Japan. However, the impact of the JDB on industrial development is questionable. After looking over the distribution of loans to manufacturing and nonmanufacturing sectors of the Japanese economy, one is inclined to agree with Japanese economist Katsuro Sakoh, who has written, "There is no evidence that manufacturing industries, in general or any particular manufacturing sector have been targeted by JDB. In fact, the share of loans that manufacturing industries have received from JDB is negligible. Industries such as iron and steel, often cited as examples of successful government assistance efforts in the early post-war period, received less than 1 percent of the loans of JDB from 1951 to 1972. This amounts to about half that received by the hotel business during the same period."[36]

Since 1972, JDB lending has shifted to urban and regional development, energy and environment. Between 1976 and 1980, almost 72 percent of JDB funds went for nonmanufacturing purposes, principally electricity, gas and water supplies (approximately 35 percent of JDB loans) and transport and communications (about 19 percent). Such statistics have caused Mr. Trezise to observe, "Effectively, the bulk of the post-1972 lending program was for infrastructure and improvements in the quality of Japanese life... If all the JDB infrastructure lending had been left to the private capital market, the economy probably would not have developed differently."[37] The targeted industries--those receiving a relatively large share of JDB funds--include agriculture, coal mining, petroleum refining and petrochemicals, shipbuilding, and aluminum, industries that tend to have considerable political influence but not necessarily great potential for growth. In developing its industrial plan in the early 1960s, the Japanese government attempted to encourage cartels among its automobile producers and to discourage Honda from going into the automobile business on the grounds that it did not have the potential to compete on the world market.[38]

Why, then, has Japan experienced so much higher growth that other countries? There are several plausible explanations.

o Taxes have taken a relatively small share of national income. In 1980 the share of Japan's national income going to taxes was 23 percent; in the United States it was 28 percent; in West Germany and France, 32 percent; in the United Kingdom, 41 percent.

o The tax system in Japan has tended to favor saving (which leads to investment and growth) and has been partially responsible for the 20 percent saving rate among Japanese workers.

o For most of the postwar period Japan has maintained a policy of balancing its budget. The growing deficits during the 1970s may partially explain the decrease in the growth rate from the 4 to 5 percent range to the 2 to 3 percent range.

o The Japanese government has had to spend little on defense.

o Wages in many Japanese industries have remained competitive. Wages in the automobile industry, for example, are approximately half what they are in the United States. An important "secret" to the ability of Japanese firms to offer their workers lifetime employment lies in competitive wages (a policy option always available to American workers). Also, the stability of employment (which tends to lower wages) in many major Japanese industries reflects the fact that 30 to 40 percent of a worker's wages is paid in the form of yearend bonuses. Such bonuses vary with the companies' profitability, which means that wages—not employment—rise and fall with the ups and downs of the business cycle.[39]

o Finally, as University of Maryland Professor Mancur Olson has argued, World War II may have inadvertently contributed to economic growth in Japan by breaking up and destroying the hold that interest groups had on government policies, reducing competition and enhancing their own profits at the expense of the general public. In other words, forced competitiveness has spurred economic growth, since fewer resources have been devoted to seeking monopoly profits through government protection.[40] Mr. Sakoh has concluded, "Ironically...the government contribution (to economic growth and prosperity in Japan) is based not on how much it did for the economy, but on how much it restrained itself from doing."[41]

MYTH 5

OUR INDUSTRIAL DEVELOPMENT PROBLEMS CAN BE SOLVED THROUGH PROTECTIONIST MEASURES AND "BUY AMERICAN" PROGRAMS.

A prominent textile executive and vocal supporter of free markets has echoed a familiar theme in the reinvigorated protectionist movement in this country: "Every time you import a product, you're exporting a job." Following the lead of others, he suggests that to solve our nation's unemployment problem, we should all "Buy American." The recently published philosophical manifestos of these born-again protectionists who have wrapped themselves in the mantle of industrial policy reveal how easy it is to overlook or ignore basic principals of international trade.⁴²

When applied to a specific industry, such as textiles or automobiles, claims of enhanced employment opportunities from protection represent special pleading, a demand that government tariffs promote the interests of the few at the expense of the many. When applied to the entire range of domestically produced goods, such arguments are absurd and lose much of their appeal even to textile and automobile workers. Nevertheless, employment claims inspired President Reagan's tenfold increase in the tariff on motorcycles in early 1983, and they undergird the emerging theory of "managed capitalism," the philosophical perspective that supports the industrial policies of Messrs. Reich, Thurow, Hart, and Bluestone.

Clearly, when domestic textile companies are unable to meet the prices charged by foreign firms, employment in American textile firms suffers. If textiles are produced abroad, textile workers are employed abroad, not in the North and South Carolina mills. Though indisputable, that fact does not mean that the total numbers of jobs in this country is reduced by textile imports. Trade—international or domestic—is always in two directions. No individual in this country will continue to sell the product of his labor and investment without expecting something in return. Similarly, no country is going to continue to sell us the products of its industry without expecting goods and services in return.

The Japanese and Koreans are willing to export to us (and allow us to import from them) for one simple reason: It is their most effective means of laying claim to the products of U.S. industries—and U.S. workers. They may sell us their textiles for dollars, but the exchange dealers seek dollars for the purpose of using them to buy American goods. The end result is that over time, imports of textiles (and thousands of other goods) give rise to (or are caused by) exports of American goods. Granted, imports of textiles may "destroy" jobs in the domestic textile industry, as proponents of protectionism argue. But because of the bidirectional nature of international trade, those imports also "create" jobs in other export sectors of the U.S. economy, a fact that those who seek protection from market competition fail to acknowledge. Many of those other jobs will be in the very states in which textile jobs, in particular, are the object of protection. If the domestic textile industry is protected, the economy's stock of jobs will not rise. Protection may lead to more textile jobs, but it will also result in fewer exports and fewer jobs in the export industries (including sectors of the textile industry that cater to foreign markets).

Nonetheless, for some very good reasons, tariffs have considerable political appeal. First, in hard times it is all too tempting to blame our troubles on others, especially foreigners who are not in a good position to defend themselves. Second, the benefits of any given tariff proposal are typically concentrated on a relatively small number of people, who because of the significant income at stake, tend to be politically active in promoting protection. The costs of each of the tariffs, on the other hand, are spread thinly over the entire consuming population in the form of higher prices and restricted supplies.

Third, the jobs that are "destroyed" by imports are highly visible. The "textile trade deficit" can be computed with ease, and the plants and workers idled because of that deficit can be readily identified--all of which can be reported vividly with pictures of closed plants and interviews with unemployed workers. The jobs "destroyed" by the protection are largely invisible to the media, which cannot disentangle job losses due to protection from job losses due to other economic forces in other countries.

Finally, protectionists have an arsenal of spurious arguments that have worked, unfortunately, to their advantage many times in the past:

o WE CANNOT HOPE TO COMPETE WITH SUBSIDIZED FOREIGN INDUSTRIES. If foreign industries are receiving extensive subsidies, as is claimed, then those companies and their workers must also be bearing a substantial tax burden, which should be reflected in the costs of their production. To develop an industrial policy that truly benefits Americans, the U.S. government should perhaps treat the subsidies much as "favorable climate," a basis for a comparative cost advantage, and exploit it. By importing subsidized products, the U.S. economy can tap into the tax base of other countries.

o UNRESTRICTED TRADE WILL WIPE OUT ENTIRE DOMESTIC INDUSTRIES. In fact, only the least efficient marginal firms will likely fall to international competition. In most major product groups, open international trade is likely to lead to greater specialization, not complete specialization.

o WE NEED OUR INDUSTRIES FOR NATIONAL DEFENSE. This appealing argument will be unconvincing until it is shown that the industries that would prosper in the absence of protection will contribute less to our national defense than the protected industries. Proponents of protectionism as part of an industrial policy must place their national defense claims in the context of comparative analysis.

o WE CANNOT COMPETE WITH THE LOW WAGES IN FOREIGN COUNTRIES. This fallacy is considered in detail below.

In evaluating the growing array of proposals for protection, consumers should recall one simple point: Such proposals come from people who have very narrow economic interests. They do not wish to be contained by the forces of competition, and they often cloak their private interests in noble claims about broader national interests—which can only rarely be validated. The honest slogan of the textile protectionist, for example, should probably be "Buy American, Save Our Textile Jobs, and Impose the Costs on Others."

MYTH 6

LOW WAGES IN FOREIGN COUNTRIES EXPLAIN THE INABILITY OF U.S. INDUSTRIES TO COMPETE WITH IMPORTS.

This protectionist position, a theme from Robert Reich's widely read book, was no doubt fortified recently when Wolfgang Hager, visiting professor at Georgetown University's School of Foreign Service, wrote:

> Without trade barriers, rich countries are bound to suck in cheap imports from low-wage countries, destroying the domestic industries that used to make those products. There will never be enough "high tech" jobs to employ those who lose more traditional jobs. Therefore, unrestricted trade would eventually destroy the economies of all high-wage, developed countries.[43]

Cheap labor is the presumed culprit for the eroding market shares of American firms in automobiles, steel, textiles, aircraft, television, robotics, and a host of other industries. Imposing tariffs, quotas, and quality controls on imports is the presumed solution that would reestablish "fair international trade" and give back to American companies their American markets.

Industrial executives ask prophetically, how can we hope to compete with foreigners who pay their workers 17 cents an hour? The answer is that we do compete. In many industrial and agricultural areas we pay high wages and export goods to cheap-labor countries, including Korea, Hong Kong, Japan, and Italy. This feat is accomplished principally where American wages reflect relatively high levels of productivity.

Although low wages may characterize the production of almost all imports, what is important is the comparative cost of production of various goods in the United States and other countries, and wages are only one factor in countries' production costs. And by comparative costs we mean not the absolute level of wages, but what must be foregone to produce some good for export.

Why? To be worthwhile, international trade must ultimately be bilateral. Moreover, wages are typically low across industries in low-wage countries. Again, no country will long persist in using its resources to produce goods for export if it gets nothing in return.

If a country like Japan exports low wage products, it must—just to make trade bilateral and worthwhile—import high-wage products from abroad. Otherwise, trade would be nothing but a drain on the economy of the low-wage country. If low wages account for imports, we must wonder how the United States could ever export anything, since our wages across the industrial board are generally higher than elsewhere in the world.

Of course, protection advocates like Professor Hager argue that unless U.S. industry is protected, all U.S. markets will be at the mercy of foreign low-wage producers--an absurd conclusion, since a foreign country's ultimate motivation for exporting goods is its demand for imports, including imports from the United States. To suggest, as does Chalmers Johnson, that "the United States is in danger of ending the twentieth century as the leading producer of ICBMs and soybeans, while the Japanese monopolize everything else,"[44] is tantamount to saying the Japanese are so stupid that they will, through exports, drain their country of its resources and get nothing in return just to achieve monopolies--a maddening contradiction of intents.

Those Japanese workers are paid in yen, and the products they produce are priced in yen. In deciding whether to import Japanese textiles, American buyers can observe only the prices of Japanese goods in yen; they probably do not care (and probably do not know) what Japanese workers are paid. They are concerned only with whether textiles can be bought at a lower cost from companies in Japan or the United States. Differences in wages and labor productivity can explain the comparative costs of products in the two countries.

To illustrate the problem facing the importer, suppose a yard of cloth costs 1 yen in Japan and $4 in the United States. That information alone, regardless of how much Japanese and U.S. workers are paid in real terms, offers little help in deciding whether textiles should be imported into or exported from the United States, since one product cannot provide the basis for bilateral trade. But say a bushel of soybeans costs 1 yen in Japan and $2 in the United States. The American importer can now reason that a yard of cloth in Japan can be made at the same yen cost as a bushel of soybeans (1 yen each), but the yard of cloth is relatively dearer in the United States ($4 versus $2).

What is important is the comparative costs of production of cloth and soybeans in the two countries. To produce a yard of cloth, Japan will have to give up a bushel of soybeans (each costs 1 yen). To produce a yard of cloth, the United States will have to give up two bushels of soybeans (one yard of cloth at $4 is worth two bushels of soybeans at $2 each). Therefore, even though wages may be low in both Japanese industries, it makes sense for cloth to be produced where the fewer soybeans are given up--in Japan. That, then, is where production tends to occur.

By the same argument, it makes sense to produce soybeans where fewer yards of cloth are forgone--in the United States. Only half a yard of cloth must be given up for every bushel of soybeans produced here, whereas one yard of cloth must be given up for every bushel produced in Japan. Indeed, the demand for yen by Americans intent on buying textiles from Japan will push up the dollar price of yen in the international money market until American soybeans become cheaper than Japanese soybeans to the Japanese.

A fundamental principle of trade, often overlooked by protectionists in their zeal to convince Congress that without protection the U.S. economy will decay into total ruin, becomes clear: Regardless of the absolute level of wages in the two countries, if the Japanese have a comparative cost advantage in the production of, say, textiles, then the United States must have a comparative cost advantage in something else, like soybeans. Again, trade must be bidirectional.

An aside: If soybeans cost $8 a bushel in the United States (and if wages remained the same in Japan), trade would be reversed. Fewer soybeans would have to be given up in Japan (one bushel) than in the United States (half a bushel), and we would export cloth and import soybeans.

One can blame low wages in Japan for the imports of cloth in our original example. But blame could just as well be attributed to the soybean industry in the United States, which is able to push the dollar price of its beans to a sufficiently low level that it, not the textile industry, is the beneficiary of the export market to Japan. The textile industry is having a difficult time competing with Japanese imports because it must compete for labor with other industries, like soybeans, that have been able to raise their productivity relative to the textile industry. As a consequence of this competitive process, the comparative cost advantage in textiles goes to the Japanese, and the textile industry is thrown up against foreign competition in its own domestic markets.

These simple but subtle analyses of international trade continue to perplex many a statesman who has been swayed by demands for protection. However, they must be understood by the voters if they are not going to be hoodwinked into greater protection, which spells higher prices and lower real incomes for Americans.

Between now and the 1984 election, industrial policy issues will attract considerable media attention. The arguments offered in support of many industrial policy schemes, however, often confuse fact and fiction. Just possibly, everyone can agree with industrial policy advocates that the United States needs a "coordinated" industrial policy, one that means government policies foster growth in jobs and incomes. But we also need to separate fact from the fiction in the debate so that citizens can understand whether a "coordinated industrial policy" should mean more or less government intervention in the economy.

NOTES

1. Robert B. Reich, The Next American Frontier (New York: Times Books, 1983), p. 3.

2. Ibid.

3. Ibid., p. 21.

4. Barry Bluestone and Bennett Harrison, The Deindustrialization of America: Plant Closings, Community Abandonment, and the Dismantling of Basic Industries (New York: Basic Books, 1982).

5. For a survey and analysis of current industrial policy proposals, see Richard B. McKenzie, "National Industrial Policy: An Overview of the Debate," Backgrounder (Washington: The Heritage Foundation, 1983).

6. Reich, The Next American Frontier, p. 20.

7. "How to Turn Recovery into Long-Term Prosperity," U.S. News and World Report (May 2, 1983), p. 52.

8. Reich, The Next American Frontier, p. 14.

9. See Bluestone and Harrison, The Deindustrialization of America; and Samuel Bowles, David M. Gordon, and Thomas E. Weisskopf, Beyond the Waste Land: A Democratic Alternative to Economic Decline (Garden City, N.Y.: Anchor Press/Doubleday, 1983).

10. Lester Thurow, testimony prepared for the House Subcommittee on Economic Stabilization (June 14, 1983), p. 1.

11. Wilson H. Hulley, "A Proposal to Form the U.S. Trade Policy Council" (Washington: U.S. Trade Policy Council, n.d.).

12. Bluestone and Harrison, The Deindustrialization of America, p. 47.

13. Joseph Badaracco and David Yoffie, "Why a U.S. Industrial Policy Will Fail," Manhattan Report (Winter 1983), p. 4. Consider also the reaction of Bruce Bartlett, economist with the Joint Economic Committee of the Congress, to concern over the impact of international trade on industrial decline: "Another misguided concern often expressed by advocates of an industrial policy is the increasing proportion of our G.N.P. devoted to imports. Though the percent of foreign goods and services sold in the United States has increased substantially over the last 20 years, United States exports have increased during the same period. Merchandise exports as a share of G.N.P. rose to 6.8 percent last year [1982] from 4.3 percent in 1970, despite the recession and a rising dollar, which increases the cost of exports. Moreover, the increase in American imports relative to G.N.P. is not out of line with other major in-

dustrial nations. While American imports of merchandise rose to 9.3 percent of G.N.P. in 1981, from 4.3 percent in 1970, Japan saw an increase to 12.7 percent from 9.2 percent during the same period" [Bruce Bartlett, "False Images and Political Bias," New York Times (June 12, 1983), p. 2F].

    14. Gary Hart, "Restoring Economic Growth," policy statement, June 1982, p. 1.

    15. John J. LaFalce, "Opening Statement," hearings on industrial policy, Subcommittee on Economic Stabilization, U.S. House Committee on Banking, Finance and Urban Affairs (June 14, 1983), p. D8.

    16. Robert J. Samuelson, "Economic Focus: High-Tech Job Binge a Fantasy," Washington Post (June 28, 1983), p. D8.

    17. Ibid., p. D14.

    18. U.S. Department of Labor, Bureau of Labor Statistics, Economic Projections to 1990, Bulletin 2121 (Washington: U.S. Government Printing Office, March 1982); see especially pp. 20-33.

    19. Of course, the employment in industries within the major sectors is projected to decline. Between 1979 and 1990 the Labor Department expects employment to decline in only 23 out of 129 industries, and no industry is expected to decline at an average annual rate greater than 3.3 percent.

    20. The conservative assumptions used by the Bureau of Labor Statistics to make its projections mean that the economic growth rates for income and employment realized in the 1970s are assumed to apply to the 1980s.

    21. Walter F. Mondale, excerpts from a speech delivered to the Industrial Union Department Legislative Conference, May 4, 1983 (Washington: Mondale for President Campaign), pp. 1-2.

    22. James K. Hickel, "The Chrysler Bailout Revisited," Backgrounder (Washington: The Heritage Foundation, July 1983), p. 2, a revised and expanded version of "Lemon Aid: Debunking the Case for the Chrysler Bailout," Reason (March 1983), pp. 37-39.

    23. Ibid.

    24. Ibid., p. 3.

    25. Ibid., pp. 9-11.

    26. Ibid., pp. 3-4.

    27. Chalmers Johnson, "MITI and the Japanese Miracle," as quoted in Katsuro Sakoh, "Japanese Industrial Policy" (Washington:

Council for a Competitive Economy, June 1983), p. 2, condensed and published as "'Industrial Policy': The Super Myth of Japan's Super Success," Asian Studies Center, Backgrounder (Washington: The Heritage Foundation, July 1983).

28. Thurow, testimony, p. 1.

29. Reich, The Next American Frontier, p. 109.

30. See Sakoh, "Japanese 'Industrial Policy,'" p. 6A; and Jimmy W. Wheeler, Merit E. Janow, and Thomas Pepper, Japanese Industrial Development Policies in the 1980s (Hudson Institute, 1982), p. 111.

31. Sakoh, "Japanese 'Industrial Policy,'" p. 7.

32. Philip H. Trezise, "Industrial Policy Is Not the Major Reason for Japan's Success," Brookings Review (Spring 1983), p. 15.

33. Sakoh, "Japanese 'Industrial Policy,'" p. 12.

34. Ibid.

35. Trezise, "Industrial Policy," p. 15.

36. Sakoh, "Japanese 'Industrial Policy,'" p. 16.

37. Trezise, "Industrial Policy," p. 16.

38. Sakoh, "Japanese 'Industrial Policy,'" p. 33.

39. Dwight R. Lee, "Mr. Reich Shows Us the Way," Journal of Contemporary Studies (forthcoming).

40. Mancur Olson, The Rise and Decline of Nations (New Haven: Yale University Press, 1982).

41. Sakoh, "Japanese 'Industrial Policy,'" p. 43.

42. Bob Kuttner, "The Free Trade Fallacy," New Republic (March 28, 1983), pp. 16-21.

43. Wolfgang Hager, "Let Us Praise Trade Protectionism: It's Free Trade That Would Bring Disaster Today," Washington Post (May 15, 1983), pp. B1 and B4.

44. As quoted in Christopher Madison, "'Industrial Policy,' Japanese Style," National Journal (February 26, 1983), p. 419.

"NIP in the Air," by Richard B. McKenzie, is reprinted from Policy Review, issue no. 26. Policy Review is a publication of the Heritage Foundation, 214 Massachusetts Ave., N.E., Washington, D.C.

CHAPTER TWO:
THE LESSONS OF EXPERIENCE

Overview

Nancy L. Johnson

There is a vision that industrial policy enthusiasts are eager to project: new and prosperous industries, leaner and more efficient factories, and unprecedented labor-management-government cooperation in a new age of American entrepreneurial leadership. The possibilities of a new industrial policy, they say, are endless, and are only limited by our willingness to adopt more innovative approaches to our economic problems.

But as the authors in this chapter illustrate, coordinated government industrial policies are in no way novel and in fact have been around long enough in other nations to demonstrate that their implementation leads only to subsidization of inefficient industries at enormous taxpayer expense. The British government's almost fruitless seven-year $3.5 billion investment in auto maker British Leyland is just one example offered in the following pages which illustrates the folly of industrial policy. Moreover, as this chapter's authors point out, many of the government-sponsored measures used in Great Britain and West Germany are the very ones being promoted for use in our economy today.

For example, industrial policy promoters in the U.S. maintain that some kind of national development bank is needed to spur growth, modernization, and entrepreneurial spirit within our domestic industries. But what would this bank do? In Britain, as John Burton--a Research Fellow with the Institute of Economic Affairs in London--points out, a similar entity--the National Enterprise Board--has doled out billions of dollars since 1975 to British companies with little or no return to the British taxpayer. In West Germany, as Klaus-Dieter Schmidt of the Institute for World Economics observes, government funds have been targeted for over a decade at declining industries, such as steel, hard coal mining, and shipbuilding, which today still remain on the brink of collapse. Would a national industrial bank in the U.S. merely prop up failing companies and establish within them an unbreakable dependence on federal subsidies?

Readers will also note that the Japanese industrial method--the model that many hold up as an example of successful industrial policy—is in fact no more than a collection of practices the U.S. has pursued for years. Brookings Institution senior fellow, Philip H. Trezise also explains that, contrary to popular opinion, Japan commits far less than the U.S. does to government-sponsored research and development, and devotes only a small fraction of government subsidies to commercialization of new technologies.

The fact that Japanese policies are merely a variation on our own measures to promote industrial growth is an important point. This finding leads to the obvious conclusion that the United States already has an industrial policy. It can be found in the vast network of federal tax credits, tax deductions, loans and loan guarantees, subsidies, contract set-asides, and international trade agreements which together constitute a conscious government effort to direct certain investment activities.

Each and every one of these special federal provisions is designed to encourage one or more types of economic activity, and a good deal of taxpayer money is expended in the process. According to the Congressional Budget Office, these mechanisms amounted to over $80 billion in federal subsidies last year.

It is hard to understand why supporters of an industrial policy want to add to this already complex and far-reaching system of government support. Already, existing investment incentives and U.S. government support mechanisms often conflict with one another. Analysts note that in 1981 the U.S. imposed import quotas on Japanese cars, but in that same year the Small Business Administration guaranteed over $6 million in loans to Datsun and Toyota dealers in the U.S. An enlightening article in The Wall Street Journal recently also pointed out that the federal government spent more than $30 billion in 1983 to prop up farm prices, and then expended $4.8 billion more for subsidized loans to foreigners so they could buy U.S. agricultural goods at below cost.

These examples highlight the need NOT for more subsidies, programs, and government influence over investment decisions, but for a more intelligent and efficient use of our existing incentives.

Finally, this chapter concludes with Richard R. Nelson's and Richard N. Langlois' assertion that many of the underlying assumptions of an industrial policy have been tested in our own country before, and have failed to yield the hoped-for results. For example, during the 1960s popular wisdom believed that high levels of government-funded research and development would spur productivity, yet the 1970s experienced a substantial slowdown in productivity growth while R&D spending continued to be high. Outright efforts by the federal government to pick winners have, as the authors note, resulted in promoting production practices or new products that have little or no commercial value.

Those who promote an aggressive new industrial policy for the

U.S. are either overlooking the experiences of other industrialized nations or are fooling themselves into believing that an American industrial policy will somehow be different than the failed measures of West Germany and Great Britain. There is probably a mixture of both of these attitudes among those promoting industrial policy, and, perhaps more importantly, there is a strong tendency, in the wake of one of the worst recessions in American history, to "do something." In this respect wishful thinking has taken hold where economic reality has left off.

Industrial Policy in Japan

Philip H. Trezise

Japanese officials, politicians, and ordinary citizens will tell you that Japan has an industrial policy. So will many outside observers, some of whom write articles, monographs and books about it. I will not quarrel with this multitude of believers.

The government of Japan does in fact devote a considerable amount of attention to the various parts of the national economy. It has institutions of long standing to facilitate consultations with private business. It has a Development Bank. It of course has the power to tax or not to tax, to protect or not to protect, to subsidize directly or not to subsidize, and so on. Periodically, it presents statements—called plans or visions of the future—which identify economic problems or technological possibilities that are considered to be deserving of bureaucratic concern and action. I find understandable the often arrived at conclusion that all these insitutions, authorities, and procedures are combined in a coherent fashion to promote Japan's economic growth and international competitiveness.

A closer look raises many doubts, however.

If industrial policy is anything more than a catch-phrase, it must mean that the government acts deliberately to assure that resources of capital and labor will go predominantly to the most promising sectors of the economy. In Japan's case, obviously, these will include, though not be limited to potential export sectors. By definition, a successful export sector must be capable of achieving international competitiveness.

Pursuit of such a policy calls for foresight or predictive skill. These are not commonplace qualities in any country. It also calls for a great deal of political forbearance. The more that public authorities have their attention diverted to backward or declining sectors, the less will be available to underwrite the chosen industries, the industries of the future as the saying goes. Yet, as experience tells us, the backward or declining industries tend to have a priority claim to political consideration, at least where popular elections are in vogue. Japan has frequent elections.

Subsidies. A straightforward way for governments to influence private economic decisions is to provide grants-in-aid, that is, outright subsidies. Most governments do so. Japan is no exception.

Who gets the subsidies? Foremost is agriculture and within agriculture the rice producing sector. Rice is produced in Japan at three to four times the price prevailing in world markets. The excess cost is shared between the Japanese consumer in high retail prices and the government (i.e., taxpayers) in price supports. Rice supports together with other subsidies make agriculture easily the most costly Japanese industry in terms of budget outlays.

Next most costly is energy. Two oil crises have made Japanese politicians exceedingly sensitive to the country's dependence on imports of energy fuels. Energy expenditures are concentrated on nuclear power--including reprocessing, the breeder, and fusion-- and on coal and oil (exploration and development, storage, stockpiling, etc.). Although these subsidies may be said to be a part of an industrial policy, the reality is that Japan's government would be spending money on energy security if the term industrial policy had never been invented.

Small business is third in line. Special assistance to this private sector is an old story in Japan. Its rationale, needless to say, is heavily political.

A large claim on the budget is exercised by the loss-making national railways. Subsidies to sustain the publicly owned rail system might be considered to be part of a carefully designed industrial policy, if one supposed that every branch line and all the members of an overmanned work force really are indispensable.

Finally, the Japanese government, like its counterparts elsewhere, finances some of the nation's R&D out of public funds. This subject deserves separate attention because of the perception abroad that Japan's public R&D spending is very large, carefully targeted, and economically exceptionally rewarding.

R&D. Large it is not. Among the principal industrial countries, Japan comes in last in terms of publicly financed R&D in relation to GNP. To be sure, only a tiny fraction of Japan's R&D budget goes to defense, as compared with, say, the 62 percent of the U.S. fiscal 1984 R&D budget submission that would be assigned to defense-military functions. Still, after adjusting for this disparity, Japan's public R&D spending is less than half that of the United States. (Private R&D, on the other hand, has surpassed that of the United States in relative terms.)

As for official R&D being meticulously aimed at commercial goals, roughly half of Japan's official spending is disbursed by the Ministry of Education, mostly to the universities as general grants for the advancement of knowledge. Since these grants are on long tether--they can be used to finance faculty salaries, libraries and administration--it is fair to put them down as being primarily funding for basic research, rather remote from industrial applications.

Another quarter of the R&D budget, more or less, goes to the Science & Technology Agency, which pays for space and oceanic R&D and for much of energy R&D.

The Ministry of Agriculture is scheduled to receive during the current fiscal year four percent of all public R&D money, twice the share that has been asked for agriculture in the U.S. budget.

One finds at the end that the Ministry of International Trade & Industry, or MITI, is to have control over only 12 percent of public R&D financing in fiscal 1983. Since more than half of that is supposed to be spent on energy R&D, the remainder is perhaps $350 million to do all the multifarious things that MITI is popularly supposed to do in the way of providing R&D in support of manufacturing industry.

Mention should be made of tax benefits for private R&D spending. Japan's tax code allows a credit of 20 percent of R&D expenditures that are in excess of the amount in the highest earlier year, subject to a ceiling of 10 percent of the firm's total tax liability. (The comparable U.S. figure is 25 percent, calculated against the three previous years' average and with no ceiling.) Also, associations formed to conduct research may write off equipment investments in the first year--an incentive for cooperative research projects.

Tax subsidies. These R&D tax provisions are among a large number of "special tax measures" in Japan's tax legislation. All of them have the intended effect of reducing tax collections so as to favor one or another kind of economic activity. In the United States, we say that these kinds of provisions lead to tax expenditures; Japan's Ministry of Finance compiles the results as "revenue losses."

The literature on Japanese industrial policy commonly attributes much significance to these selective tax benefits. Selectivity is there all right, but not quite as advertised. All manner of tax benefits are provided--accelerated depreciation, increased initial depreciation, tax free reserves, tax exemptions, tax credits, and depletion allowances--but the beneficiaries can hardly be said to have been selected because they are uniformly industries of the future. The restaurant industry, food processing, textiles, paper and pulp, non-ferrous metals, agriculture, mining, forestry, and merchant shipping enjoy or have enjoyed special tax favors, along with steel, chemicals, certain machinery sectors, and other more commonly remarked candidates. Investors in housing built for renting have long benefited from accelerated depreciation allowances. Today robotics investors are similarly treated. So are airlines when they buy new planes (which Japan does not produce).

Not only are special tax measures for the industrial-business sector a hodgepodge but the total amounts at issue are surprisingly small. The Ministry of Finance calculates that in fiscal 1981 the gross revenue losses from all special tax measures were about 1100 billion yen, say, $5 billion. Half of this was attributable to various small savers' exemptions, as on interest earnings from bank deposits under 3 million yen. Another one-fourth was the result of such things as tax benefits for doctors whose fees from the social insurance program are considered—by the doctors—to be unduly parsimonious. The remainder, something over a billion dollars, was spread over all of Japan's business world. Comparisons may or may not be wholly fair in these matters, but it is at least worth remarking that Office of Management and Budget estimates of U.S. tax expenditures for fiscal 1984 include as only one of the line items a figure of $14.6 billion for the investment tax credit and certain related tax benefits for industry.

The Japan Development Bank. Japan has a second budget, known as the Fiscal Investment & Loan Program (FILP). It is financed out of postal savings and other fiduciary deposits with the government and is disbursed in the form of loans at concessional rates. Some students and journalists have found in it one of the keys to Japan's economic successes. Viewed more soberly, the FILP is a Japanese parallel to our tax-free federal, local and state bond issues and the Federal Financing Bank. FILP lending goes for the most part to local governments, housing, highway corporations, regional development projects, and so on. That these kinds of activities are funded more cheaply than in the private market is hardly uncommon among advanced industrial countries.

Something less than a third of the FILP is handled by several corporations or banks that are empowered to lend directly to what would be customarily considered private business sectors. Their lending mandates run principally to small business and to agricultural, forestry, and fishery enterprises. The exceptions are the Export-Import Bank and the Japan Development Bank.

Like its American counterpart, the Ex-Im Bank helps to finance big-ticket exports. (This financing, incidentally, is the only important remaining export subsidy.) As in the United States, the Japanese Ex-Im has had one major customer, in its case the shipbuilding industry rather than the aircraft industry. It seems right to say that the Ex-Im Bank serves an industrial policy purpose. But it would not be right to call it distinctive, for all of Japan's major competitors have a similar lending institution.

The industrial policy literature tends to single out the Japan Development Bank as the central instrument of industrial policy. The JDB has had as its mission "to promote industrial development and economic and social progress." Its lending program in fiscal 1981, representing new authority and repayments of old loans, was 1.0 trillion yen, or about $5.1 billion. Many commentators assert that its loans have a multiplier effect because the evidence of governmental interest tells private bankers that a JDB borrower should be given preferential treatment. (Why this should be true in present-day Japan is not altogether clear.) Unlike the small business lending institutions, which actually are far more generously endowed, its customers in principle are to be found in the big business and prospectively high growth sectors.

Examination of the lending program makes for some doubt about the JDB's role in industrial policy. Of the $5 billion scheduled to be disbursed in 1981, $2 billion was earmarked for energy projects. About $700 million was to be allocated to urban development—private railroads, modernization of distribution facilities, and urban renewal. Regional development lending was set at $760 million. Quality of life loans—pollution prevention, safety measures, food supply, city gas—were to be $560 million. The merchant marine industry, a perennial claimant for JDB assistance, was to get $550 million.

These parts of the program—about 88 percent of the whole—have to do, basically, with economic infrastructure. It may make the best of sense to nurture private infrastructure projects with public loans at interest rates somewhat below commercial rates, although an argument can be made that the Japanese flag merchant marine at least is more a burden than a boon for the national economy. But to find in these JDB operations a highly focused form of industrial policy is simply not possible.

Of the remainder of the $5.1 billion, the 1981 program proposed loans of $475 million for the "development of technology"—that is, computers, the electronics and machinery industries, and R&D. These loans, and perhaps the $145 million of "other" lending, may fit well with the conception of a national policy aimed at the economic future. But the total of $620 million, in a country where private plant and equipment investment was running (1981) at something like $180 billion, does not look to be a decisive force for shaping the future.

<u>Protection</u>. Throughout the 1950s and 1960s, Japan's import policy can be characterized as protectionist. It was protectionist for infant industries and more established industries alike. Because foreign exchange control was the principal instrument, and the balance of payments the rationalization, import restrictions even extended to many goods not produced in Japan at all. This wholesale protectionism was a factor in the growth and diversification of Japan's economy in those decades. Whether it was all necessary or always well calculated is open to question, but it

was in any case the fact.

After the liberalization of the 1970s Japan now stands as a country with generally low tariffs, processed foods and certain semi-manufactures aside, and relatively few other official barriers to imports, agricultural goods excepted. Formal, official protection, in other words, cannot be said to be a significant feature of industrial policy.

It is often alleged that the private sector itself runs a protectionist regime through informal buy-Japanese or buy-only-within-the-industrial-group practices. The extent to which this allegation is accurate cannot readily be established. If private protectionism is indeed widespread and the sums involved substantial, then Japanese business must willingly be passing up important potential gains from international trade. This does not seem consistent with the abundant evidence of vigorous inter-firm competition in Japan. And if industrial policy relies in important measure on a self-defeating practice (so far as profit maximization is concerned) then perhaps the policy's merits will need to be reconsidered.

Competition policy. It is certainly true that Japan does not have a Sherman Act tradition. The Fair Trade Commission, a pro-competition inheritance from the postwar occupation, has survived and in recent years been strengthened somewhat, but the general thrust of official thought in Japan has been toward worry about "excessive" competition and toward a possibly exaggerated faith in economies of scale. Thus, industry laws and government policy have emphasized ways to limit competition and to foster bigness. What we have learned recently about official measures to organize cooperative R&D in semiconductors comes within this intellectual and policy framework.

To be sure, much of the drive to restrict competitive excesses has been directed at sectors like textiles, where entry is easy and small firms come and go with great frequency. The record suggests that the policy has been less than fully effective. Small firms are as numerous as ever in, for example, the clothing industry, which has long engaged the attention of MITI's textile bureau. A sizable official effort in the automobile parts industry during the late 1950s and early 1960s may have had greater success; but here the major auto producers must have had an important role as they went about developing reliable supplier relationships.

The machine tool industry, also a target for nationalization programs, appears still to be one of relatively small firms whose competitive positions are subject to rapid change.

In a few industries, particularly shipbuilding and petroleum refining, investment decisions have had to be formally approved by government authorities. In others, such as steel, the government has sometimes intervened to defer capacity expansion projects.

Price leadership in steel has been allowed and in fact fostered by the official establishment. Cartels to manage export restraints have been frequent, as have so-called recession cartels.

Nonetheless, the government's competitive policy writ does not run without limit. In the 1960s, MITI made a famous bid for broad powers to guide and rationalize designated industries, beginning with autos, specialty steel, and petrochemicals. The auto industry, MITI officials believed at the time, could best be organized into only two groups centered around Nissan and Toyota. This proposal attracted much business, bureaucratic, and political opposition. Eventually it was abandoned. More generally, it seems clear, Japanese business and industry have been able to evade or ignore many of the rules, restrictions, and guidances that it has found unhelpful. Much of Japanese economic life is visibly rivalrous, not only in the small firm sectors but also in autos, electronics, and other industries where big companies dominate.

Currently, the MITI version of competition policy is being applied, in modified ways, to a group of "depressed" industries which include aluminum and certain petrochemicals and chemical fertilizers. These are mostly industries which have been hurt by high energy prices and which stand in need of more or less severe capacity reductions, or so it is agreed. Legislation enacted in 1978, and revised and renewed this year, gives the government ministries, in most cases MITI, authority to guide and induce the necessary adjustments. The usual formula is to get agreement on scrapping of capacity under some form of fair shares arrangement, and then to promote various kinds of joint action in the way of production, marketing, or raw material procurement.

This is truly a version of an industrial policy: the government steps in to help organize a process or orderly disinvestment when an industry is judged to require downward adjustment. Whether this will prove to be more economic than a policy of leaving everything to market forces is open to question. The worst-case aluminum industry has already shut down more than two-thirds of its 1978 capacity and is still shrinking; a less intrusive MITI policy might have seen the reduction accomplished even more quickly, to the general benefit. But the actual approach probably conforms to prevailing Japanese views, and is not plainly wrong-headed.

All in all, it is difficult to find in Japanese competition or anti-competition policies anything fitting within an overall industrial policy. Some sectors of industry and business are populated mainly by small firms, where atomistic competition to some extent prevails. Others are in varying degrees oligopolistic, in some cases with governmental blessing and support. There is certainly no standard pattern, designed by central authority.

Plans and visions. An industrial policy would seem to call for a plan or blueprint to provide guides for day-to-day and month-to-month implementation. These are not evident in Japan.

Every now and then, usually after a new prime minister takes office, the Economic Planning Agency and its advisory body prepares a multi-year Economic and Social Plan. "Plan," however, is a misnomer. These documents resemble rather our President's annual Economic Report to the Congress. They discuss trends and problems, economy-wide and in some cases sectoral, and suggest broad courses of action, often heavily qualified (because a number of ministries have a hand in the preparation). To draw the particulars of a focussed industrial policy out of the Plan would require an enormous amount of freehand exegesis.

MITI and its senior advisory council also prepare a plan, or "vision," which is nominally more narrowly confined to the industrial part of the economy. In fact, past visions have been very discursive statements, ranging over many subjects not all of them strictly within MITI's purview, the exchange rate for instance. But they do provide a check list of specific technologies and products that are believed to hold out promise for the future. Government interest in these is justified very much as the OMB explains federal support for R&D--that the private sector may lack incentive to invest adequately on its own.

That certain technologies receive mention in the visions does not mean that their commercialization is assured. Or if it does, then Japan infallibly will achieve nuclear fusion on a commercial basis in some finite period. The London Economist has said that the futuristic technologies cited in the visions are mostly "fantasies." This may be too deprecatory a term, but it is certainly no further from fact than the notion that inclusion in the MITI list is equivalent to a guarantee of successful development.

Concluding comments. As a nation, Japan clearly has done many things right. The recovery from wartime devastation and disruption and the subsequent record of economic growth were impressive achievements by any standard. No single source or cause explains these accomplishments. Government was one of the contributing factors, but only one among many. And its principal contribution arguably was in prudent macroeconomic policy making (with one major lapse in 1972-1974) rather than in the detailed interventions that are now supposed to amount to a closely articulated industrial policy.

The belief that the government supports the winners--and discards the losers--is in conflict with reality and, for that matter, with common sense. One of the chosen industries is the aircraft industry. It has been the object of special promotional legislation and close bureaucratic guidance and nurturing since 1954. It is still a small industry, overwhelmingly dependent on a single captive customer, the Japan Defense Agency. One of the laggard sectors is clothing. Per capita value added in this industry is the lowest in all manufacturing. During the 1970s, when total employment in manufacturing declined, employment in the clothing industry increased.

Automobiles represent one of Japan's spectacular industrial successes. An industry that produced 165,000 inelegant and high cost cars in 1960 is now the world's leading producer and, as is well known, the leading exporter. Its biggest export market, to state the obvious, is the United States, where mass production of was invented. Some of the public comment about this phenomenon could be taken to suggest that it was planned and "targeted" by some extraordinary prescient people a couple of decades ago.

Prescience in the automobile instance would have required a prevision of the oil crisis of 1973-74, for it was this event that led to the surge of Japanese exports to the United States. From the late 1960s to 1975, Japanese exports had been increasing, but almost entirely at the expense of European suppliers. It was only after the gasoline shortages and higher gasoline prices that the Toyotas, Datsuns, and the rest began to take the market share away from Detroit. To believe that anyone anywhere foresaw all this is to believe anything.

In short, happenstance as well as good quality, good marketing, and competitive prices had its part in this Japanese miracle, as it had in the larger economic growth miracle. MITI and other ministries of government played parts also and it would be pointless to argue that these were irrelevant or negative. It is equally wrong, however, to attribute to MITI and to something labelled "industrial policy" the principal credit for accomplishments that were the product of complex and shifting combinations of forces and events. Above all, it is wrong to assume that Japan's mix of policies, which on inspection proves not to be a coherent whole anyway, has some valid application to our own, made in America problems.

From testimony before the Joint Economic Committee, July 13, 1983. Reprinted by permission of Philip H. Trezise.

West Germany: Another Industrial Policy Victim

Klaus-Dieter Schmidt

For nearly three decades after World War II, West Germany was the showcase of the Western market economies. Growth rates were consistently higher and inflation and unemployment were lower than in most other countries. This phenomenal postwar takeoff—sometimes called a miracle—has often been ascribed to a favorable supply of production factors. West Germany, for instance, inherited from the Third Reich a structure of industrial capacity which faced a highly elastic demand at home and abroad and benefited from an ample supply of trained labor. But that is not the whole story. A good part of the success was due to the contribution of a strongly free market economic policy. West Germany's economy was simply more market-oriented than the economies of most other countries.

Since the early 1970s, however, the situation has changed dramatically. Like other Western industrialized economies, West Germany began to experience a pervasive and sharp slowdown in economic growth. Advances in Asian economies and the upward revaluation of the Deutsche Mark have altered drastically the unique position of West German industries in domestic and world markets. This change has been particularly painful for the West German textile, clothing, shipbuilding, and steel industries.[1]

The causes of this decline seem to be clear: high labor costs and poor productivity. Had West Germany reacted to this problem with the same free market approach that characterized its early postwar history, the nation's industry would no doubt be undergoing a painful, but ultimately successful, period of restructuring. Unfortunately, it broke with the past, and adopted the seemingly easier approach of industrial policy. The result should serve as a warning to those who flirt with the same ideas in the United States—industrial policy does not lead to adaptation, it merely puts off the day when changes must take place, and makes the inescapable transition even more difficult.

GERMAN INDUSTRIAL POLICY

To be sure, the West German government has reacted to the weakening economic performance by relying predominantly on market forces. Chancellors Willy Brandt and Helmut Schmidt were guided by the pragmatically non-interventionist rules of the postwar "social market economy." Nevertheless, growing unemployment and seeming deindustrialization produced a demand for more state intervention. The government faced pressure from the shrinking industries—from both owners and trade unions.

Intervention has been a constant companion of the basically market-oriented West German economic policy in the last two decades.[2] Under the principles of this policy, established by the federal government in the late 1960s, intervention was considered acceptable in three cases:

o to counter the effects of subsidies of other countries,

o to correct market failures in the domestic economy, and

o to support the process of structural change.[3]

The objective of such structural adjustment, according to the Act of Stability and Growth, is defined as the "promotion of productivity and growth of enterprises or branches, especially by innovation of producing methods." But a review of the assistance provided shows that there is a big difference between goals and reality. The industries that have benefited from this industrial policy are almost without exception raw materials and raw material intensive products. Most of these are declining industries that are inefficient or overmanned, such as coal mining, steel making and shipbuilding. What is euphemistically called "adjustment" is, in fact, pure maintenance aid. Support has been given to labor intensive branches as if they were industries of the future.

Maintenance has often been justified by the aim of tiding an industry through lean times. But the West German experience supports the view that the trouble with "temporary measures" is that they have a habit of becoming permanent. The problems besetting the West German coal-mining industries, for example, are still much the same as they were before intervention started in the late 1950s.

The West German government's industrial policy was portrayed as a well thought-out intervention in the marketplace. The application of the policy, however, has been quite chaotic. An exhaustive enumeration would be an arduous undertaking, but the following measures provide a disturbing picture of industrial policy in practice.

Trade Protectionism. There has been a marked shift to subsidies and—especially in recent years—to tariff setting. This has been due to a decline in nominal tariff rates implemented in the Kennedy and Tokyo Rounds of trade liberalization, which have encouraged financial and nonfinancial protection tailor-made to the problems of specific industries or regions. In manufacturing, for instance, the effective rates of domestic subsidization as a percent of value-added climbed from 2.7 percent to 3.7 percent in 1981, while the rate of tariff protection, which in 1974 amounted to 10 percent, declined to approximately 6.5 percent.[4]

Subsidies to Major Industries. The European Economic Community (EEC) was established, in part, to encourage harmonious and integrated development among the European nations. The EEC, however, has not prevented a subsidization race among European governments. The West Germans entered this race by granting subsidies on a large scale to the steel industry and other declining industries. By 1981, coal mining, steel making, and shipbuilding were receiving 42 percent of all subsidies to manufacturing, up from 25 percent in 1973.

There has been another interesting change in the pattern of support in West Germany. Before the 1970s, selective aid was granted to protect whole sectors. In more recent years, however, far more emphasis has been laid on specific unprofitable or bankrupt firms--in clear breach, incidentally, of the official guidelines of structural policy. The government has undertaken a considerable number of rescue operations. The case of the Frankfurt electrical engineering firm AEG was but one recent example, and the impending bankruptcy of the Saarbrucken steel producer ARBED dominates the headlines of West German newspapers.

It is remarkable that the approach of supporting national "champions" has never been an important part of West German industrial policy. The supposed Japanese strategy of "picking winners" has always had some disciples, but they are in the minority. There have, of course, been some examples of efforts to support new industries, but they are unusual. In the early 1970s, for instance, government was engaged in building up a national computer industry, but the program was a flop. At present only two new industries are financed on a large scale by the taxpayers--the aircraft industry and nuclear energy. The results have not been a major success. Even the allegedly successful Airbus program is currently in need of increasing subsidies, although D.M. 400 million was provided in 1980.[5]

Technology. One important component of government's intervention in West Germany is the promotion of technology research. In 1981, government spent D.M. 8.5 billion (8.4 percent of all subsidies) on R&D programs. R&D support, in contrast to general support, has been directed more toward growth industries. Funding of R&D in industry, however, has been concentrated on just a small number of industries, in particular aircraft manufacturing and specialized mechanics--with the notable exception of chemicals and biotechnics. In addition, the bulk of public R&D funding goes to a small number of large corporations: in 1979 six firms received 44 percent of the funds distributed by the Federal Minister of Research and Technology. Only a small fraction of public support (mainly tax relief) is open to all firms. Indeed, West German technology policy discriminates against emerging small and medium-sized firms, which are less able to deal with the bureaucratic maze.

Mergers in Declining Industries. In contrast to the tradition of West German competition policy--a fundamental element of the "social market economy"--the approach of encouraging the merger of firms has become a common feature of policy in recent years. This change began in 1969 with the founding of the Ruhrkohle AG, a state-owned holding company for the depressed hard coal firms of the Ruhr. In the late 1970s, the state strongly influenced the concentration process in the aircraft industry. The merger between MesserschmidtBolkow-Blohm and the Vereinigte Flutechnische Werke, for instance, was orchestrated by the federal government. Several recent efforts have been undertaken to bring weak firms under the same industry roof in both the steel and the shipbuilding industries.

Why the government and other proponents of industrial policy favor such a solution is not quite clear. Presumably they believe that the restructuring of a depressed industry can better be handled if the industry consists of a small number of giant firms. The experience of the Ruhrkohle AG, however, shows the opposite to be true. From 1958 to 1969, productivity in the hard coal industry doubled. But since the formation of the state-owned company in 1969, no significant increase has been registered.

INDUSTRIAL POLICY AND OVERCAPACITY

A full assessment of the extent of government intervention in West Germany is not easy, but it appears widespread and considerable. Nobody can really tell where an industry would stand had there been no subsidies, tariff protection, or other nonfinancial aid. But the evidence suggests that the results of West German industrial policy are unencouraging. In the case of the three industries that have been the principal targets of industrial policy --hard coal mining, steel making, and shipbuilding--the contrast between goals and reality could hardly be more striking.[6]

Hard Coal Mining. By the late 1950s, West German hard coal mining reached a dead end. The fuel was able to compete neither with other fuels nor with foreign hard coal. Subsidies did allow the price for West German hard coal to be forced down to the world market price, yet they could not stop the decay of West German hard coal mining. Production declined from 150 million tons per year during the early 1950s to 90 million tons per year by the 1980s. During this period, the number of employees declined from 500,000 to 200,000, and unsold stocks reached 45 million tons a year. Subsidies for West German coal mining not only led to overcapacity but also heralded a rise in costs. Labor and social insurance costs in mining are the highest of all West German industry.

The Steel Industry. The West German steel industry currently is struggling for existence. Steel products are too expensive, reflecting high production cost and low productivity. Moreover, there is considerable overcapacity due to the shrinking worldwide demand for steel.

The West German steel market, like that for hard coal, is a controlled market. In 1963 it was separated from the world market by the High Commission for Coal and Steel: tariffs on imports from third countries were raised, imports from countries with government-controlled economies were limited, and a minimum price system was introduced in the domestic market. Steel companies also obligated themselves "voluntarily" to observe certain delivery dates and guiding prices on the domestic market. Many agreements were made with Third World countries on quantity and prices concerning imports of steel to the EEC. In 1980 the steel companies had to accept production quotas for crude steel and rolled steel, and registration with a controlling system was required. In 1981 production quotas for other steel products were implemented, and the control of prices was intensified.

The regimentation of the steel market is now complete. Companies are told what quantity of steel they can produce and the minimum prices they must charge. There are de facto import controls and quotas, and import prices may not be lower than the basic domestic price.

The steel industry case is an excellent example of how the government's attempts to achieve structural changes were counterproductive. Enterprises could rely on the fact that, in times of economic weakness, declines in prices and production would be compensated. Consequently, companies were encouraged to invest more than otherwise could have been profitable. Since 1970 the production capacity has increased by 15 percent, while production actually decreased by 15 percent.

The Shipbuilding Industry. Like coal and steel, West German shipyards are not suffering so much from declining demand as from competition from foreign suppliers. The big shipyards, which specialized in building tankers and bulk goods freighters, are lagging behind the shipyards of Japan and South Korea.

The West German shipbuilding industry was at its peak in the late 1950s. At that time the Howaldtswerke in Kiel was the most important shipyard in the world, and six West German shipyards were among the 50 largest in the world. The crisis began in 1961, when the Schlieker shipyard got into difficulties, and the first pleas for government aid were made. Since then West German shipbuilding has received enormous subsidies. Every ship now built in a West German shipyard is one-third financed by the government.

These measures have not helped the process of adjustment. On the contrary, they have delayed it. Overmanning persists. Since the mid-1970s, production has decreased by two-thirds, but employment only by only one-quarter. The shipyards have still to face the fact that they must scrap the excess capacity built up in the early 1970s with West German taxpayers' money.

CONCLUSION: TOWARD AN INDUSTRIAL MUSEUM?

Advocates of industrial policy in West Germany put forward three standard arguments. Such policies, they say, can provide emergency relief when the market is turbulent. They can be used to shield industry from unfair foreign competition, and they can be used to moderate market distortions.

None of these arguments is convincing on the basis of the West German experience. For example, hard coal is distributed throughout the world, and competition among producers is strong. Emergency relief, therefore, could be provided better by buffer stocks than by a policy of permanent excess productive capacity.

Advocates of industrial policy, moreover, usually underestimate the distortions they impose on the allocation process when calculations are made outside the market—when the costs associated with getting subsidies are lower than those for earning market incomes. There is, indeed, strong evidence that the structural problems appearing in the 1970s were the result of an increase in intervention, not the reason for that intervention.

West Germany is by no means being overwhelmed by a wave of protectionism. Firms and workers express the view that the government should fight for open markets—but also for trade barriers against "unfair competition." Enterprise associations, like the Bundesverband der Industrie (BDI) are therefore in a quandary: They have to uphold the free trade interest of the export sector and yet also advocate the protectionist interests of the domestic import-substitution sector. Consequently, producers' associations generally recommend trade barriers only when the export interests of West German industry as a whole are not likely to be endangered by countermeasures.[7]

In contrast with the industrial policy debate in other countries—for example, the United States and France—the idea of revitalizing the economy by an industrial policy has only a few advocates in West Germany, but this may be changing. Government intervention can seem very attractive when a society is unwilling to face the pain of industrial adjustment. Economic history provides numerous examples of such situations. And even though intervention has failed to bring about orderly and rational change, politicians seem bent on killing the goose that lays the golden egg.

The dangers implicit in adopting an interventionist industrial policy to allay painful change were noted in 1940 by the famous German economist August Losch: "The forced immortalization of formerly useful interests, and in particular the complete preservation of the former state, creates a museum, which like any institution of such a kind, requires considerable costs of upkeep. Very often it would be better to facilitate the disentanglement of the old combination of country, people and activity and to search for a new combination, that means to promote adjustment instead of hampering it."

The West Germans are at the point of turning their economy into an industrial museum, thanks to a misplaced enthusiasm for industrial policy.

Notes

1. See Klaus-Werner Schatz and Frank Wolter, International Trade, Employment and Structural Adjustment. The Case Study of the Federal Republic of Germany. International Labor Office, Geneva, World Employment Research. Working Papers, October 1982.

2. The term industrial policy is not used in German. The equivalent would be structural policy (Strukturpolitik), which is relatively unknown in Anglo-Saxon language. Structural policy comprises all government interventions that affect the inter-industry allocation of resources.

3. Organization for Economic Cooperation and Development, Transparency for Positive Adjustment. Identifying and Evaluating Government Intervention. Paris 1983.

4. Frank D. Weiss, Industrial Policy and International Competitiveness in West Germany (unpublished).

5. Equal to $160 million, assuming $1 = D.M. 2.50.

6. See Klaus-Dieter Schmidt, et al., Im Anpassungsprozess zuruckgeworfen--Die deutsche Wirtschaft von neuen Herausforderungen. Kiel 1983.

7. In a highly developed country like West Germany, however, intra-industry trade plays an important role. Any given industry, subindustry, or even firm will be likely to export and import. The West German textile and clothing industry is the world's largest exporter and one of the largest importers. Quite a few firms have tried to escape wage costs pressure by reallocating production in East European countries. An ideal vehicle has been subcontracting. About one-seventh of total imports of textiles and clothing are re-imports after offshore processing.

From the Heritage Foundation's International Briefing, March 7, 1984. Reprinted by permission of the Heritage Foundation, Washington, D.C.

Britain's Industrial Policy: Valuable Lessons for the U.S.

John Burton

Many of the major developments in American domestic economic policy over at least the past half century seem to have been copied from actions in the United Kingdom. Where Britain has led, America has often followed. The pump-priming New Deal Keynesianism and the more full-fledged Keynesian policies of the Kennedy-Johnson years, for instance, were foreshadowed by the Keynesian revolution in the U.K. The wage-price guidelines of the Kennedy-Johnson period and the incomes policy control and phases of the Nixon Presidency were preceded by innumerable British experiments, dating back to 1948.

This pattern is once again being repeated. Over the past year many influential American voices have called for a national industrial policy for the United States.[1] The analyses of these American advocates of industrial policy are based, implicitly, on one of two presuppositions. Some seem to think they are proposing radically new policy initiatives, as yet untried elsewhere. Others suggest that the adoption of selected industrial policies has been the foundation underlying the postwar economic success of Japan.

The latter supposition is in general quite untrue. While postwar Japanese governments have experimented with some selective targeting of industries, this has generally been of a low-key nature and not aimed at Japanese manufacturing.[2] The hallmark of postwar Japanese policy toward industry instead has been the provision of a general (as against selective) policy climate (through low government spending and taxation) that was conducive to industry, entrepreneurship, innovation, and investment.

More important, U.S. policymakers and citizens should recognize that the recent industrial policy proposals for America have for long been preached, and endlessly experimented with in practice, in Britain--well before attention was given to the Japanese model. All of the "new" buzzwords of industrial policy--adjustment assistance to "sunset" industries, financial assistance to promote new "sunrise" industries and technologies, the establishment of tripartite (business, union, and government) councils to improve cooperation, and many others—have been heard and enacted in Britain over the past 30 years. Even industrial policy advocate Felix Rohatyn's recently unveiled idea for a "social compact" between management, government, and unions turns out to be a hand-me-down from the Labor government of the late 1970's—a compact which in reality gave a free rein to the unions. There is nothing new about the "new" debate on national industrial policy in the U.S. It is all old hat in Britain.

The British experiences with industrial policy thus are valuable lessons about the probable effects of an industrial policy in the U.S.[3] Advocates of such an approach can take little comfort from the British track record. Far from bringing about an industrial rebirth, it has led to expensive but unsuccessful bailouts, the creation of losers out of one-time winners, spectacular high-tech projects that are also spectacular money losers, and an erosion of business freedom. Perhaps worse of all, the British experience shows that the process may well be irreversible.

BRITISH INDUSTRIAL POLICY IN THE POSTWAR ERA

Industrial policy is centuries old in Britain. The Navigation Acts of 1651 and 1660 provided English merchant ships with a monopoly of imperial trade, and such discriminatory British economic policies were an important factor leading to the revolt of Britain's North American colonies.

Under the shadow of 20th century world depression, Britain again adopted a protectionist commercial policy between the two World Wars after a century of free trade. Additionally, the government began to support certain sectors of industry. This support was supposed to encourage industry to rationalize by amalgamation and eliminate "competitive waste," to close inefficient firms, and to improve the industrial structure.

But protective tariffs, far from regenerating the economy, "encouraged resources to flow to the least dynamic sectors of British industry, and so slowed down the shift from the 'old' to the 'new' by distorting the allocation of resources."[4] The measures did little to effect economic recovery—indeed they hindered it.[5]

Neither did industrial support bring forth a regeneration of industry. Rationalization promoted by government led most often to restrictions on the entry of new firms into an industry and price fixing within it. "Industrialists...were probably keener to accept the subsidies, restrict competition, and fix prices, than to reduce capacity."[6] Economic revival did eventually come, but it owed nothing to such government measures. The recovery was based primarily on newly emerging industries, not on industries restructured with government aid.

The most immediate impact on industry of the Labor Government of 1945 was the state takeover, or "nationalization," of many basic industries, including coal, electricity, gas, railways and canals, civil aviation, overseas cable and wireless, and the Bank of England (iron and steel were brought under state ownership in 1951 under the second postwar Labor Government). This experiment in state ownership of the "commanding heights of the economy" has proved to be an unmitigated and expensive disaster for the British taxpayer. Over the period 1945 to 1979, government subsidies to the nationalized industries have totaled approximately $45 billion (at 1979 prices). Nationalization as an industrial policy has proved to be merely an excuse to run large parts of the economy as if these industries were a sheltered workshop for politically powerful workers. New financial "disciplines" on the nationalized industries laid down by Parliament —in 1961, 1967, and 1978 in particular—have failed miserably to bring about improved financial performance.

Efforts by the Conservative government of the early 1950s to return state industries to private hands proved politically ineffective and short-lived. Indeed, the pace of government involvement accelerated in the 1950s and 1960s. Even Conservative administrations found themselves unable to untangle the network of aid and controls.

Government subsidy schemes toward industry multiplied and changed at a dizzying rate. It is no exaggeration to say that by the mid-1970s British industrial policy had become a subsidy morass.[7] Nor, with the exception of some "touches of the tiller" of industrial policy, has this situation changed fundamentally since Mrs. Thatcher came to power in 1979. Britain provides an important and salutary case study in the apparently irreversible and suffocating effects of industrial policy.

INDUSTRIAL POLICY IN THE 1960s

The Lure of National Planning. In 1962 the Conservative government sought to achieve higher growth by the establishment of a new institution, the National Economic Development Council. This NEDC was supposed to harness government and "both sides of industry" and to take responsibility for the provision of long-term plans and forecasts.

A comparison between the targets set out in NEDC reports and the actual course of the economy indicate that the tripartite council failed totally to achieve its targets. "Between 1961 and 1966 total output rose by 2.9 percent a year, compared with the NEDC target of 4 percent. Productivity appeared to grow no faster than in the previous five years...manufacturing investment grew by 0.2 percent a year, compared with the target of 3.3 percent."[8]

Despite the lackluster results of such indicative planning, the incoming Labor government of 1964 was inspired to intensify the experiment by establishing a new Department of Economic Affairs (DEA) with responsibility for overall medium and long-term indicative planning. Eleven months later, the DEA produced a National Plan, which was "a mixture of forecast, feasibility study, policy directive, industrial targetry and a dissertation on the economic facts of life."[9] The NEDC target of 4 percent a year growth was replaced by one of 25 percent growth over 1964-1970 (about 3.8 percent a year). Again, the theory was that, by indicating the beneficial implications of higher growth, the higher growth could somehow be achieved. The basic assumption, as before, was that the growth rate could be "talked up."

In July 1966 the National Plan was abandoned in the wake of a sterling crisis; but it is difficult to see that much could have come of it in any event. Industry in general was skeptical of the growth target. To quote one commentator: "Looking at the forecasts in retrospect, it would be interesting to know how many companies felt that they were less in the dark...than they were before."[10]

The White-Hot Technological Revolution. The Labor Party's 1964 election platform promised to transform the British economy by means of a government-sponsored "white-hot technological revolution," meaning:

> a deliberate and massive effort to modernize the economy; to change its structure and to develop with all possible speed the advanced technology and the new science-based industries with which our future lies.[11]

A number of government initiatives were undertaken toward this end. In 1966 the Industrial Reorganization Corporation (IRC) was established, with the task of promoting selected mergers with taxpayer finance, where such a change in industrial structure would lead to greater efficiency. The Corporation was responsible for a number of developments, its two largest efforts being the GEC/AEI merger (where the Corporation supported an oppposed takeover) and the merger between British Motor Corporation (BMC) and Leyland to form British Leyland. An important study by the Brookings Institution concluded that the IRC's basic strategy was to "find the most efficient firm in Britain and merge the rest of them into it."[12]

It was predictable from the beginning that such government-initiated mergers would not necessarily lead to a more successful, or even viable, enterprise. The classic illustration of this is the sorry history of the British Leyland Motor Corporation (BLMC), the major British auto assembler, brought about by an IRC-supported merger, in 1968, between BMC and Leyland Motors. Far from creating a larger, successful enterprise, BLMC subsequently lurched toward bankruptcy, the cost of avoiding which fell to the IRC's successor in the mid-1970s.

Arguably, there was at least one success in the IRC's portfolio of government-promoted mergers--the formation of GEC from English Electric and AEI. Out of the 70 cases the IRC handled in the four years of its life, however, this would be a rather solitary success. But even in that case, the IRC's involvement was scarcely crucial. As one study of the overall performance of the Commission has concluded, the results "do not make a distinguished list."[13] Although the IRC was expected to earn a commercial return overall on its operation, it in fact provided funds to private companies at way below the price on the capital market for comparable projects. As another study notes "in many cases it is doubtful if the borrowers (from the IRC) would have been in a position to obtain funds at any interest rate"[14]

The Reasons for Failure. Why did the IRC perform so badly? First, there was an inadequate appreciation of the simple fact that even the most efficient firm may not remain so if it has to carry the weight of less efficient organizations chosen by a government agency. Second, although the IRC was staffed by people from the private sector, it was not realized that businessmen, who have been transformed into salaried bureaucrats handling other people's (taxpayers') money, behave differently from their former private sector colleagues.

The IRC was only part of the package of industrial policy measures sponsored by the British government in the late 1960s. Sectoral policy for high-technology industry found its expression in legislation passed in 1965. The purpose of this was to support high-risk R&D projects, on the grounds that they generate diffuse benefits for the whole economy, and to accelerate the introduction of technological innovations in industry. Later, the Industrial Expansion Act of 1968 was designed "to promote efficiency; to support technical advance; or to create, expand or sustain productive capacity" with injections of taxpayer money into selected firms and industries. This legislation was subsequently used to facilitate mergers in the British computer industry, to establish a primary aluminum smelter industry in the U.K., and to make large loans and credit guarantees to the Concorde jetliner and the cruise ship QE II projects, among other ventures.

Did these measures bring about the promised "white-hot technological revolution?" The evidence suggests not. Britain's new computer firm, International Computer Limited, formed in 1968, fell into acute financial difficulties in the mid-1970s and again in the early 1980s. On both occasions, it was bailed out by government injections of cash and guaranteed loans. Yet it never performed as well as had been promised by industrial policy advocates. And the subsidies given to create a primary aluminum smelter facility led to an even more glaring financial fiasco. As one study in 1977 concluded:

> one smelter has yet to make a profit and the other two have yet to achieve an adequate return...the eventual

cost to the taxpayer could be nine times as much as was first thought.[15]

The drift of industrial subsidies to levels well beyond those initially contemplated is a recurring pattern in the story of recent British industrial policy.[16] Yet it should be noted that "for a long time [industrial] policy was seen as a model of anticipatory intervention."[17] In other words, it was assumed in British governmental circles that the aluminum smelter subsidies and similar instances of support demonstrated that government, acting as an entrepreneur with taxpayers' money, could make better judgments than could those involved in industry. The dismal history of such ventures tells another story.

The Anglo-French Concorde supersonic jetliner project illustrates another danger with industrial policy: the allure of "high tech" to political decision makers, who fail to consider the economic and business criteria for assessing technical developments. The Concorde plan was developed, at enormous cost to the British and French taxpayers, on the supposition of their governments that such a jetliner would allow their aircraft industries to get "one generation ahead" of U.S. airplane manufacturers. And high-tech the Concorde assuredly is; but commercial it is not--a quality well understood by independent financial analysts long before its production. The cost per seat mile of the Concorde is roughly three times that of the Boeing 747. British Airways, the national flag carrier, even refused to purchase any of the airplanes until it was assured that it would be compensated by government of the inevitable losses. Sales or even interest outside the manufacturing countries has been practically nonexistent.

The "white hot technological revolution" of the latter half of the 1960s is now mainly remembered for its creation of costly white elephants. The British taxpayer is still paying for many of them.

INDUSTRIAL POLICY IN THE 1970s

The Shift Into Top Gear In June 1970 a new Conservative government under Edward Heath came into power with a mandate for less government and the "disengagement" of government and industry. Specific pledges included the abolition of the IRC; a reduction of government spending on industry; and a promise by the new government's industry minister that he would "not bolster up to or bail out companies where I can see no end to the process of propping up." This pledge became known as the "(no) lame ducks policy."

The IRC was indeed duly abolished in May 1971, and the Industrial Expansion Act of 1968 was repealed. The refusal to support lame duck industries with taxpayers' money also seemed to be holding fast. In 1970, for instance, the government refused to give bridging to the ailing Mersey Docks and Harbour Board, and it withdrew financial support from the British film industry. It also abstained from financing or subsidizing a proposal for nuclear merchant vessels.

The attempt to "disengage" from industry, however, began to falter by 1971. Under media and political pressure, the government stepped in to support four failing Scottish shipyards and agreed to continue subsidies initiated by the previous Labor Government.

Another major dent appeared in the lame ducks' policy, thanks to the financial collapse of Rolls Royce at the end of 1971. This company had been urged and heavily subsidized, under the policy of the previous Labor government, to develop the RB-211 jet engine, which had been chosen by Lockheed to power its L1011 "Tristar" wide body jetliner. Very large cost overruns in the engine's development, combined with an inflexible contract on the engine's price, threatened corporate bankruptcy for Rolls Royce. In February 1971, the government stepped in and the major part of the company was nationalized as Rolls Royce (1971) Limited. Large amounts of taxpayers' money followed.

The early experience of the Heath government showed that, once industries come to expect government subsidy, it becomes very difficult for government to withdraw from an active industrial policy.

In 1972 the initial retreat from the disengagement philosophy became an about-face. In a crisis atmosphere of 5 percent unemployment, the government completely reversed its economic policy. A new commitment was made to monetary-fiscal laxity and intensified levels of industrial subsidization, in order to promote expansion.

The 1972 Industry Act conferred wide powers on the British government, enabling it to assist financially selected firms and industries. To the embarrassment of the Conservative government, the foremost of Britain's left-wing politicians, Tony Benn, hailed this Act as the most socialist measure ever passed by Parliament. Under the Act, grants, loans, and equity acquisition could be used to assist projects to create employment and for modernization and nationalization schemes in industry. An Industrial Development Advisory Board (IDAB) was created to give advice on industrial problems to the government and to consider major cases for selective assistance with taxpayers' money. An Industrial Unit (IDU) was also created, which seemed to many to be little more than a reincarnation of the IRC.

The 1972 Act, passed by the Conservative government, thus opened the floodgates once again. Among the industries receiving aid were shipbuilding, mainframe computers, textiles, machine tools, and motorcycles, all of which exhibited clear lame duck characteristics.

Labor returned to power in 1974, committed to extensive industrial policy measures to reverse the "deindustrialization of

Britain." This so-called New Industrial Strategy was given legislative content by the Industry Act of 1975. Among other things, the Legislation created the National Enterprise Board (NEB), bankrolled with approximately $1.5 billion[18] of taxpayers' money. This was a new state agency that could lend to and acquire stock in private sector enterprises. It was charged with two objectives—which proved to be incompatible.

1) The promotion of industrial efficiency and international competitiveness,

2) The provision, maintenance, or safeguarding...of employment.[19]

The problem was that while objective (2) is the long-run consequence of pursuing (1), the attempt to prosecute (2) in the short-run, by industrial subsidies, undermined (1) by thwarting the market process of economic evolution. As one economist put it, there was a built-in danger of putting the cart of employment preservation before the horse of economic efficiency.[20]

Banking Losers--British Leyland. The conflict between these two objectives of the NEB was nowhere more plain than in its attitude toward British Leyland, the auto manufacturer created by the IRC in the 1960s. During the first half of the 1970s, problems intensified within the company, ranging from a lack of good engineers, through atrocious labor relations, to a failure to develop designs for future models. By 1975 the company was heading for a crash, and a study team was set up by the government to report urgently on the matter. The eventual report, known as the Ryder plan,[21] called for an injection of about $1.5 billion of taxpayers' money, over the period 1975 to 1982, in order to allow British Leyland to reequip and regain commercial viability. The government, fearing the economic collapse of the West Midlands of England--Britain's auto engineering region--if British Leyland was not saved, committed itself to the plan and took over most of the shares of the company, which were then transferred to the NEB.

In fact, the allocated money had been spent within British Leyland by 1980, whereupon a further $450 million of equity was injected by the NEB in 1980-1981. In January 1981, the Secretary of State for Industry announced a further transfusion of nearly $1.5 billion of taxpayers' money during the next two years.

Despite these vast injections, British Leyland continued to lose the equivalent of hundreds of millions of dollars each year, while total government support for the company, via the NEB, topped $3.5 billion, or about $60 for every man, woman, and child in Britain. As Grylls and Redwood have noted, this was "one of the biggest and costliest rescue operations ever mounted in U.K. industrial history."[22] The financial return to the taxpayer has been zero, and the volume of government finance eventually committed proved to be well over double that envisaged in the original

Ryder rescue plan. Nor is there yet much sign that the corporation will ever get back into the black.

It has been argued that the reorganization of British Leyland would have proceeded at a much faster pace, with a keener appreciation of the urgency of the situation, if government support had not been so generous. It could also be argued that the $3.5 billion spent on the company would have created far more employment if taxpayers had been left to spend the money themselves. As one study has noted, "Sir Michael Edwardes (the chief executive) departed at the end of 1982 leaving a company far more vulnerable to closure or break-up than the concern he took over in 1977."[23]

While the NEB was saddled with two major companies with difficulties—British Leyland and Rolls Royce—by political pressure, its ability to "pick winners" is described by one study as follows: "the return of a loss on capital employed of over ($450 million) in businesses where the NEB (did have) autonomy is somewhat disappointing."[24]

"Sectoral Schemes" and "Planning Agreements". The second major element of the New Industrial Strategy of 1975 was the implementation of an overt corporatist framework for government and industry discussions. The idea was to "bring together the interests of all concerned"—large companies, large trade unions, and government—so that "Industry and Government are explicit partners in a close relationship."[25] At the level of each main industry, sector working parties (SWPs) were established, composed of representatives from management, unions, and government. By 1979, approximately 40 sectors of manufacturing industry had SWPs, reflecting about 40 percent of total manufacturing output. A new array of industrial subsidies, known as "sectoral schemes" was established, linked to the plans of the SWPs. Under each scheme, government grants were available for reequipping, rebuilding, rationalization, and restructuring in the chosen sectors, but recipient firms had to try to find alternative employment for any redundant workers. Industries covered in this way included electronics, components, machine tools, clothing, ferrous foundry, nonferrous foundry, poultry meat processing, red meat slaughterhouses, textile machinery, paper and board, printing machinery and wool textiles. By 1979 some $375 million of taxpayers' money had been allocated to this clutch of sectoral subsidy schemes, amounting to about one-fifth of the average costs of each project so covered.

These arrangements exemplified the corporatist style of much economic policy in the U.K. at that time.[26] One of the basic problems with such policy approaches, however, is that they tend to unite manufacturers and unions against competition, and for government subsidies, but to unite them on very little else.

No figures have been published on the returns to the taxpayer, or to society generally, from these sectoral schemes (some of which still continue), so an overall assessment is impossible. But this merely points to another general problem with industrial policy: the more diverse and diffuse subsidy schemes become, the greater is the difficulty of assessing their impact or of providing the taxpaying public with an impression of how wisely its money has been spent.

A third element in the New Industrial Strategy was the concept of a "planning agreement," whereby enterprises would be required to provide government with information for planning purposes and to harmonize their business activities with national planning objectives. This system of planning agreements was originally expected to cover the largest 100 or so U.K. manufacturing firms, together with all state enterprises, in a compulsory planning agreements framework. The 1975 Industry Act, however, made planning agreements voluntary. Only one company, Chrysler U.K., which had received $85 million in grants and $75 million in loans to continue in operation, signed such a planning agreement (a condition of the subventions being made).

By the late 1970s, the variety of subsidies available to enterprises, especially those in the "Assisted Areas" (supposedly economically backward regions), had become so extensive that it took a 44-page booklet simply to list them.[28] Moreover, the Assisted Areas by then covered the greater part of the surface area of the country, and the total assistance available could often add up to three-quarters of the outlay on set up costs in these areas. Targeted industrial subsidy schemes had become a subsidy morass available to practically everyone.

It is not at all clear, however, that this sophisticated and extensive apparatus of industrial policy had any influence in improving overall economic performance. Over the period of 1974-1978, the rate of growth of productivity in the U.K. was on average a meager 0.8 percent per annum (excluding the distorting effects of North Sea oil revenues), compared with 3.2 in West Germany, 3.0 in France, and 3.4 in Japan.[29] Indeed, by ossifying the structure of firms in favored industries and sectors—at considerable tax and other costs to those not favored by the selective measures—it may well be that economic performance was actually depressed by the policy. A basic problem with assessing industrial policy, of course, is that once it is in place, there is no way to know what might have happened in its absence.

INDUSTRIAL POLICY IN THE 1980s

The Thatcher government, which took office in 1979, did not come to power with a detailed philosophy regarding industrial policy. Its rhetoric suggested, however, that the Conservatives would make a more substantive attempt to disengage government from industrial policy commitments than was the case under Edward Heath. In 1980, Conservative ministers began to describe this new policy direction as "constructive" industrial policy.

Yet constructive industrial policy has not been much of a revolution. The sums of public expenditures allocated to industry by government remain just as high in real terms as under Mrs. Thatcher's predecessor. Moreover, approximately two-thirds continues to go to "sunset" industries.[30] All the Thatcher government has really done so far is to trim the tiller of industrial policy. Regional aid has been pared down, and more new expenditure goes to small businesses and to information technology developments. Otherwise, little has changed.

IMPLICATIONS FOR THE U.S.

Some very basic lessons can be drawn from the British experience with industrial policy:

1) There has been a long and sustained attempt to pick "winners" by means of industrial subsidies. But this has not led to a better economic outcome than in countries, such as the U.S., that have not adopted industrial policies. In 1980, for instance, output per employee in U.S. manufacturing was approximately 2.5 times that of the U.K.[31]

2) The supposed "winners" have shown an alarming tendency to turn into costly "losers" for the taxpayer. British Leyland, in particular, has become a basketcase, despite high hopes and billions of taxpayer dollars. And the "wonder plane," the Concorde, has been a boon to rock stars and business tycoons, but a pain to the British taxpayer.

3) Related to the second point, it appears to be extremely difficult for government—even a new government explicitly committed to a new direction of policy—to reduce the level and extent of industrial policy subsidies, once they have been initiated.

These matters deserve pondering before the U.S. embarks upon a national industrial policy. Advocates of the strategy seem determined to give the U.S. public the rosiest picture possible of the industrial policy track record. They keep citing Japan—as though it were the only country ever to have experimented with the idea—and even in the Japanese case they are highly selective in the evidence they choose to utilize. But the advocates say nothing of the sorry history of industrial policy in countries such as France, Italy, or Britain. Small wonder.

Notes

1. These proposals are outlined and examined by R.B. McKenzie, "National Industrial Policy: an Overview of the Debate," Heritage Foundation Backgrounder No. 275, July 12, 1983.

2. For a detailed debunking of the Western mythology surrounding Japanese industrial and trade policies, see K. Sakoh, "Industrial Policy: The Super Myth of Japan's Super Success," Heritage Foundation Asian Studies Center Backgrounder No. 3, July 13, 1983; and G.C. Allen, How Japan Competes (London: Institute of Economic Affairs, 1978), Hobart Paper 81.

3. For more extensive discussions, see J. Burton, The Job-Support Machine: A Critique of the Subsidy Morass (London: Center for Policy Studies, 1979); and J. Burton, Picking Losers: The Political Economy of Industrial Policy (London: Institute of Economic Affairs, 1983), Hobart Paper No. 99.

4. F. Capi, "Protectionism—No Solution to Deindustrialization," Economic Affairs, October 1983, p. 24.

5. F. Capi, Depression and Protectionism (London: Allen and Unwin, 1983).

6. A. Skuse and R. James-Owen, Government Intervention and Industrial Policy (London: Center for Policy Studies, 1979).

7. See J. Burton, The Job Support Machine: A Critique of the Subsidy Morass (London: Center for Policy Studies, 1979).

8. A. Budd, The Politics of Economic Planning (London: Fontan, 1978), p. 100.

9. R. Bailey, Managing the Economy (London: Hutchinson, 1968), p. 69.

10. Ibid., p. 77.

11. Labor Party General Election Manifesto, London: The Labor Party, 1964.

12. R. Caves, et al., Britain's Economic Prospects (London: Allen and Unwin, 1968), p. 321.

13. M. Grylls and J. Redwood, NEB (London: Center for Policy Studies, 1980), p. 8.

14. G. Denton, S. O'Cleireacain, and S. Ash, Trade Effects of Public Subsidies to Private Enterprise (London: Macmillan, 1975), p. 23.

15. C. Jones, The L200,000 Job (London: Center for Policies Studies).

16. See the later references to British Leyland and the British Steel Corporation in particular.

17. S. Wilks, "Liberal State and Party Competition: Britain," in K. Dyson and S. Wilks (eds.), Industrial Crises: A Comparative Study of the State and Industry (Oxford: Martin Robertson, 1983), p. 129.

18. Throughout this paper, amounts of money in pounds sterling have been converted to dollars at the rate of L1 = $1.50.

19. Sixth Report on Competition Policy (Brussels: Commission of the European Industry, 1978), p. 163.

20. V. Curzon-Price, Industrial Policies in the European Community (London: Macmillan, 1981), p. 58.

21. British Leyland: The Next Decade (London: HMSO, 1975).

22. Grylls and Redwood, op. cit., p. 55.

23. British Leyland, op. cit., p. 26.

24. S. Wilks, op. cit., p. 148.

25. An Approach to Industrial Strategy (London: HMSO, 1975), Cmnd. 6315.

26. Another major aspect of the corporatist approach was the "Social Contract" between the Government and the unions, whereby the unions were given a direct say in the formulation of economic policy, in return for their accession to an incomes policy.

27. F. A. Hayek, The Road to Serfdom (London: Routledge and Kegan Paul, 1944), p. 30.

28. Incentives for Industry in the Areas for Expansion (London: HMSO, Department of Industry, 1976).

29. G. Hutton, Whatever Happened to Productivity? (London: Institute of Economic Affairs, 1980), p. (iii).

30. In early 1981 the Government announced a "reconstruction of the finances of the British Steel Corporation (a state enterprise) involving a write-off of a cool $5.3 billion of taxpayers' money invested in the Corporation. The Government also announced further aid of $1.25 billion in 1981-1982."

31. National Institute of Economic and Social Research Review, August 1982, p. 29.

From the Heritage Foundation's International Briefing, March 7, 1984. Reprinted by permission of the Heritage Foundation, Washington, D.C.

Industrial Innovation Policy: Lessons from American History

*Richard R. Nelson
and Richard N. Langlois*

Government involvement in the research and development (R&D) process has a long history in this country. As is too often the case, this rich experience has seldom been consulted in policy debates over government programs to stimulate industrial innovation.

This article is an attempt to identify some of the lessons of past federal R&D policy. It summarizes the conclusions of a study, recently completed at the Center for Science and Technology Policy at New York University, of how such policies have shaped technological change in seven major American industries—semiconductors, computers, aircraft, pharmaceuticals, agriculture, residential construction, and automobiles.[1] What makes this study unique is its explicitly comparative, cross-industry focus: it was predicated on the hypothesis—amply supported in the resulting case studies—that the kinds of government programs that have shown themselves feasible and effective vary greatly among industrial sectors, depending upon the nature of the governmental involvement and the nature of competition in the industry.

The selection of industries for study was made with an eye toward obtaining a sample with a broad spectrum of characteristics: industries with fragmented as well as with concentrated structures, and industries subject to much government intervention and to relatively little. The design of the study was also informed by a desire to attract recognized scholars knowledgeable about the technology in each industry: the prior interests and areas of expertise of these scholars were therefore a factor in the selection of industries. The study was then carried out as a cooperative research effort.[2]

THE UNRAVELING CONSENSUS

In treating the questions of innovation policy as warranting detailed empirical exploration, we were acknowledging, reluctantly, that the general theoretical analyses and statistical observations of economists provide only limited and incomplete guidance for policy. We are not alone in this perception; the most significant aspect of the recent economic literature on innovation is its progressive inconclusiveness about the appropriate role for government.

It was not always that way. Economic research a decade or more ago had settled on two closely related sets of propositions about industrial innovation. The first of these was that technological change is an important source of productivity growth and, simultaneously, that R&D expenditure is a principal determinant of technological advance. The implication drawn from this was that R&D spending is a kind of "control variable" through which one would affect macroeconomic productivity.

The second set of arguments is derived from theoretical rather than statistical work. Economists during the 1950s and '60s developed models in which private firms possessed an inherent tendency to "underinvest" in R&D. There were several reasons for this unhappy circumstance: (i) R&D creates knowledge, and knowledge is a "public good" in the sense that the firm cannot fully appropriate to itself the benefits of the knowledge it creates;[3] (ii) the payoff to R&D is uncertain, and risk-averse firms will therefore wish to do less of it than a (risk-neutral) society would prefer;[4] and (iii) the fragmented structure of certain industries militates against sufficient R&D spending, the firms being too small to undertake certain kinds of projects.[5]

Taken together, these sets of arguments strongly supported the notion that the government's role lay in correcting a global problem of inadequated private R&D. But over the last decade the consensus surrounding this conclusion has essentially come undone.

First, and perhaps most important, the experience of the 1970s cast doubt on the presumed tight link between a nation's overall R&D spending and it state of productivity growth. Although it is true that high rates of R&D spending attended the rapid growth of productivity in the United States, Western Europe, and Japan during the 1950s and '60s, spending for R&D continued to be high in most countries during the ubiquitous slowdown in productivity growth after 1973. Only in the United States and France was the slowdown presaged by a decrease in R&D expenditures, and in both those countries the decrease was almost exclusively in defense and space rather than in civilian areas. Moreover, recent studies of the differences in productivity growth among countries suggests that, even in the 1950s and '60s, the countries with the highest ratio of R&D spending to gross national product—the United States and Great Britain—had among the lowest rates of productivity growth.[6]

Part of the message seems to be that it matters where a country is relative to the frontier of technology and productivity. Countries not on the frontier can "play catch up" fairly easily without much R&D spending so long as their rates of physical investment are high. Countries nearer the frontier have to work harder for each percent increase in productivity. This begins to suggest that it is not necessarily to a country's great advantage to be alone on the frontier. There is evidence that, as before World War II, the United States is again benefiting from technological ideas developed elsewhere; and there may be much to recommend a world in which many countries share the technological frontier and therefore share a common economic environment in an interdependent way.[7]

At the theoretical level, many economists have also begun to believe that the relationship between competition and innovative behavior is more than a matter of some tendency to "underinvest" (or even to "overinvest") in R&D. The relationships of innovation to information "externalities," to risk, and to market structure are increasingly seen to be subtle and complex.[8,9]

In the first place, the implications for total R&D spending of imperfect appropriability are now understood to be less clearcut than they once seemed. Economists are coming to realize that, in a world of patents and industrial secrecy, firms in some instances have an incentive to engage in duplicative or nearduplicative R&D in an effort to copy a rival's technology or "invent around" its patents. This at once calls into question the idea that firms necessarily engage in too little R&D; more important, it begins to focus our attention not on the level of R&D but on the types of R&D projects the industry engages in.

The economist's view of the "uncertainty" issues had taken a similar turn. Rather than focusing on the amount of R&D that uncertainty is likely to draw forth, economists are now recognizing that what uncertainty really demands is the exploration of a diverse set of approaches. This way of looking at things suggests that heavy commitments to any one approach are dangerous in the early stages of development of a technology and should be avoided until the uncertainties (both market uncertainties and technological ones) are significantly reduced.

What that suggests in turn is that the focus of the policy issue should shift from R&D levels to the portfolio of R&D projects an industry tends to generate. This entails turning our attention toward the incentive effects of policies and institutional structures and toward considerations of access, secrecy, and information flow. In practice, some kinds of R&D projects will tend to be "underfunded" and some to be "overfunded"; and a simple R&D subsidy is not the sort of policy such a situation demands.

THE CASE STUDY APPROACH

Although many economists are exploring new approaches to the theory of innovation and technical change, analyzing the effects of government policy on industrial innovation must still be seen as largely an empirical problem--which policies have worked, which have not, and why. This was the premise behind our seven industry case studies. One conclusion, which we develop below, is that what the government can do effectively differs from industry to industry. There are nevertheless certain features common to technological change in all industries that should be kept clearly in mind in designing government policies.

One theme that unites the history of technological change is the pervasiveness of uncertainty. Although it takes a form in (say) the pharmaceutical industry very different from that in the commercial aircraft industry, uncertainty seems nevertheless to be endemic. A quick reading of the case studies is enough to dash any supposition that technological change is somehow a cleanly plannable activity. In fact, it is an activity characterized as much by false starts, missed opportunites, and lucky breaks as by brilliant insights and clever strategic decisions. Only in hindsight does the right approach seem obvious; before the fact, it is far from clear which of a bewildering array of options will prove most fruitful or even feasible. Strange as it now seems to us, aviation experts were once divided on the relative merits of the turboprop and turbojet engines as power plants for the aircraft of the future; and the computer industry was by no means unanimous that transistors--or, later, integrated curcuits--were to be the technology of the future. Policy must recognize uncertainty as a fact of life, and must not try to repress it or analyze it away.

A second and related universal theme is the importance of detailed knowledge of the technology, of its strengths and weaknesses, and of user needs in guiding the innovation process. In all the case studies, either the producer-provider or the user-demander played a major role in generating and screening technological advances. Whenever major innovation was attempted without access to their knowledge, the results were disastrous. This fact imposes severe constraints on what government can do effectively.

The implications become clear if we consider four general kinds of government support for civilian R&D: (i) programs attendant on government procurement or some other well-defined public objective; (ii) programs to support research on "generic" technologies--research in the gray area between basic scientific research and applied R&D; (iii) programs to support applied R&D in the service of well-defined clientele demands; (iv) programs that insist on "picking winners" in commercial applied R&D. Programs of each sort show up in several guises in the industry case studies.

PROCUREMENT-RELATED R&D

In three of the industries studied--aviation, computers, and semiconductors--the government was heavily involved as a user-demander of the technology. This kind of government involvement has two important policy implications.

The first has to do with the ability of the government to guide R&D effectively. In cases of government procurement for defense, space, or similar clearly defined public projects, the government is itself the user-demander. It thus has knowledge of its own needs and, usually, at least a modicum of expertise in the technology it proposes to use. Motivation and knowledge line up fairly well in such circumstances, and the government is frequently able to sponsor effective R&D on the relevant technology. To the extent that the technology can be easily transferred to commercial application, the result is the well-known "spillover" into civilian technology.

Second, a public belief in the legitimacy of the government's primary mission—defense, for example—smooths the political waters for any related program of government R&D support. In the semiconductor industry the Department of Defense and the National Aeronautics and Space Administration (NASA) played a crucial role. Both the transistor itself and the integrated circuit were first developed with private funds; but, in the latter case at least, military and space demand was certainly an important motivation, and once those innovations were clearly identified, government support of product and process engineering helped speed their advance. Similarly, the government funded much of the early research, and provided much of the early market, for the digital computer. Defense procurement and in recent years heavy government R&D funding have played a major role in the evolution of aircraft technology.

It is important to recognize that the efficacy of government procurement-related R&D depends on the knowledge-advantage that comes from the government's position as user and on the political legitimacy of its mission as justified on the grounds other than spillover benefits. The conclusion thus does not extend to government procurement projects, the justification of which is the spillover itself or in which the procurement is intended to make a market for the technology. [The supersonic transport (SST) project remains the best case in point.]

Moreover, our case studies suggest that the potential for the generation of spillover by procurement-related government R&D support may be limited to the early stages of a technology's development, when the government and civilian demands are not yet specialized. As a technology matures, the requirements of the government and the private sector normally diverge. This means not only that spillover diminishes but also that military and commercial R&D increasingly compete for resources. In the mature phases of a technology's development, spillover may be as much to the military from the commercial sector as the other way round.

GENERIC TECHNOLOGIES

When there is no recognized public-sector demand for a technology, the government's ability to fund R&D effectively and to guide the development of that technology is more limited. The government does not then have natural access to the sorts of information necessary to guide allocation, and may in fact be blocked from getting the information. Furthermore, the legitimizing effect of a public sector purpose is not there to protect a support program from strong political opposition.

Nonetheless, these problems may be attenuated if the government restricts its attentions to areas, such as the so-called generic technology, that are a step or two removed from specific commercial application. The reason is that, at this "directed basic" level of research, the knowledge involved has a large public component: much of it is the sort of nonpatentable and nonspecific knowledge--broad design concepts--that is generally shared among scientists and does not pose a strong threat to proprietary interests.

In a sense, such generic work falls in between the sorts of work that an academic researcher, pursuing fashionable questions within the bounds of standard scientific field, would tackle and the kinds of result-oriented research that would interest most corporate R&D laboratories. Of course, some companies do support generic research, and the findings are very often treated as public rather than as proprietary. In many instances, the findings for such research comes at least in part from governmental sources. In either case, the keys to success seem to be, first, involving the relevant scientific and technical communities in the allocation process and, second, recognizing that research ought to be influenced both by the purely scientific disciplines and by those interested in applications; indeed, a tension between the pure and the applied is generally salutary.

Our case studies provide examples of generic research, some associated with government procurement (in aviation, computers, semiconductors) and some more commercially oriented work (certain aspects of agricultural and pharmaceutical science).

The agricultural sciences, viewed as a generic research system seem to have defined and filled their niche appropriately. Such work fits in between the academic basic sciences (like chemistry and biology) and the applied R&D carried out in private firms and in the experiment stations (like the development of new seeds or fertilizers). Interests on both sides of the line pull and tug to influence the kinds of research that are done as well as to monitor its quality and efficacy. The biomedical research community is another example. Research here too is pulled by applied interests (the physcians) and tugged by scientists in the more basic fields. Interestingly, both the agricultural and the biomedical sciences typically reside in university settings, but in separate professional schools rather than main-line departments.

Another similarity between agricultural science and biomedical research is the way funding allocation is carried out. Both disciplines take the majority of their support from the government, but the funding agencies keep their distance, allowing the allocation machinery to be manipulated by the research communities themselves.

The National Advisory Committee on Aeronautics (NACA), the forerunner of NASA, is another example of a generic research system. Here the setting was a freestanding organization, not a university. But NACA's research concerns were certainly generic—broad-gauged aviation problems rather than specific designs—and the relevant engineering societies played a significant role in guiding and monitoring work at NACA. After World War II, the military increasingly assigned to private contractors the sort of work NACA had carried out, a trend that both reflected and abetted the divergence of military from civilian aircraft technology.

Because generic research poses a diffuse rather than a visible threat to established competitive positions, it may be possible to mount such a program successfully in any industry. But the size of the gray area between the basic and the applied may vary greatly among industries. Of course, the extent of this generic range may be influenced by the presence of a government program: the public financing of R&D often proves contagious, luring business scientists into a wider communications network and increasing the public flavor of private work. This is certainly desirable to the extent that it does not diminish the private incentive or ability to seize upon new ideas and develop them for market.

The manner in which a generic program develops may also be of critical importance. The aborted Cooperative Automative Research Generic Technologies Program (COGENT) of the last administration seem to fit the description of generic systems, yet neither attracted the enthusiasm of the industries it proposed to aid, perhaps because the initiative and the design of the programs came strictly from Washington, with little participation by industry.

CLIENTELE-ORIENTED APPLIED R&D

The most important characteristic of government support for basic and generic research is that it does not require government administrators to make decisions that involve considerations of profitability and commercial potential. A basic or generic research program seeks to advance scientific and technical knowledge. While acquiring this sort of knowledge is not a trivial matter, it can at least conceivably be marshaled by program administrators, especially since the the relevant scientific community can often be enlisted to help guide allocation. Moreover, basic and generic research, which involves exploring widely applicable technological options, seldom poses a concentrated threat to proprietary interests.

When we move closer to the level of applied research, however, the problems of government involvement multiply. The knowledge involved is both specific and idiosyncratic in form and may be proprietary in character. This instantly puts the government administrator at an informational disadvantage vis-a-vis firms that have no incentive, and sometimes no ability, to transmit what they know to Washington. Moreover, it is difficult to maintain a political constituency for a program that poses visible threats to established competitive positions.

Now, there is one much-discussed example of a strikingly successful government program of applied R&D: the agricultural research system. As noted above, much of the research supported in this program has been basic and generic, but a sizable proportion has been extremely applied in character, focusing on particular objectives like better seed varieties or most effective pest control. The interesting question is: what special conditions have made this applied R&D program feasible and productive?

A crucial factor of the agricultural industry is that it is largely atomistic in form. The competition among farms is something near to the "perfect competition" described in economics textbooks rather than the more rivalrous kind that characterizes most manufacturing industries. For this reason, fellow competitors are seen as inherently less threatening in farming than in other industries; technological knowledge is therefore far less proprietary, and there is a public cast to the results of even very applied R&D.

The federal-state system of agricultural experiment stations evolved in a way that took advantage of the market structure in agriculture, marshaling the support of the farmers and giving them an important position in the evaluation and selection of projects. Coupled with the regional nature of agricultural technology, this led to a system in which farmers see it advantageous to them to advance even very specific technologies as quickly as possible. As a model for the administration of a government-supported applied R&D program, the agricultural system is quite instructive. It is highly decentralized, and specific resource allocation decisions are made at state and county levels. Those decisions respond with some sensitivity to the demands of two constituencies; farmers (given voice through state legislatures) and the agricultural scientific community.

In the language of the social scientist, we might call this a "captured" system, in much the same sense that transportation, communication, and other industries are said to have captured their regulators. Capture of this sort is not very often congruent with the general interest of consumers; but in the case of agriculture the system seems to have evolved in a salutory fashion.

The residential construction industry is also relatively atomistic in structure, and has therefore long been seen as conformable to the agricultural model. Yet several government efforts to spur housing R&D have not worked: more accurately, the housing industry beat back or cut back the government attempts to mount such programs.

There are probably many reasons for the nontransferability of the agricultural model to housing. Building is somewhat more rivalrous in character than farming, at least at the level of materials suppliers. More important, the atomistic home builder is very likely more conscious of a threat from housing innovation than is (or was) his counterpart in farming. Although agricultural innovation did in the long run lead to the demise of the small farmer by increasing the scale of farming operations, each small farmer could nonetheless see the benefit to him (in the short and medium run, at least) of improved farming methods. The builder may well be more aware that any exploitation of scale economies brought about by innovation would very likely rebound to his disadvantage, posing a clear threat to the system of small local firms in which he operates. Another factor is that building codes—a very old form of "new social regulation"—are intractable and entrenched. And there is not the background of good basic science in housing that there is in agriculture.

Beyond that, however, it may have been crucial that the agricultural research system evolved slowly over time and was not constructed de novo or centrally designed. It may even be that its success derives critically from the particular path the system's development followed (for example, its growth out of what was essentially a training program for farmers) and particular historical circumstances (such as the characteristics of the 19th century industry) that are not easily replicated.

PICKING WINNERS

This brings us to the final approach to government R&D support—"picking winners" in commercial competition. Here the historical record seems, for a change, unequivocal. Unequivocally negative.

The SST project and Operation Breakthrough were two examples touched upon in our case studies. In both cases, the government did not attempt to create a framework in which scientific and user interests could guide allocation: rather, the federal agencies attempted to insert themselves directly into the business of developing particular technologies for a commercial market in which they had little or no procurement interest.

In the case of Operation Breakthrough, the Department of Housing and Urban Development had been neither a major builder nor a buyer of nonsubsidized housing. It had been neither the technical expertise nor the market experience that commercial success demands. Similarly, the government was not in the business of making or buying commercial airplanes; those who were, the commercial aircraft companies, showed little interest in such a plane until the prospects for high subsidies appeared. Very few of the housing designs that came out of Operation Breakthrough have since had any commercial value; and the lesson from the British-French Concorde experience is that we are lucky we went no further than we did with the plans for an American SST.

The lesson here is not specific to these cases; it is not that these particular government agencies lacked some necessary expertise that could in principle have been remedied by hiring a larger or better cadre of experts. The lesson is a general one, about the location of knowledge and the mechanism of its transmission in the R&D system.

European experience testifies to the generality of the lesson.[10] In many cases, government attempts to enter the business of commercial applied R&D led to (i) duplicating private efforts or (ii) subsidizing those efforts and thereby replacing private with public funds or (iii) investing in designs the private sector had long abandoned as unpromising. There is certainly an argument that the government can be more forward looking than a private firm, supporting projects that are uncompromising today but may be promising tomorrow. But the most effective way to perform such a next-generation function is not by competing in the commercial marketplace but through research of a more generic sort.

LESSONS FOR POLICY

The conclusions of a comparative historical analysis can only be qualitative and judgmental. But perhaps the lesson of economic theory and political practice during the last couple of decades is precisely the importance of this sort of empirical analysis.

Our central conclusion might be summed up in one word: complexity. The wide diversity of technological and institutional details, of knowledge structures and incentive structures, among American industries recommends against an industrial policy to boost "industrial innovation" in some global sense in the hope of affecting macroeconomic problems. Broad-brush measures like tax policy, which affect each of the various industries in a very different way, should be assessed on their own merits and should not be viewed as "control variables" to stimulate innovation.

We do not propose a general rationale or justification for active government support of R&D. Applying the lessons of history to create programs that are both politically viable and socially desirable is no straightforward task. But the historical experience we have examined reveals three approaches that have worked in the past: support associated with government procurement or some other well-defined public sector objective; support of defined nonproprietary research, with allocation funds guided by the appropriate scientific community; and provision of an institutional structure that allows potential users to guide the allocation of applied R&D funds.

A fourth kind of policy, whereby government officials themselves try to identify projects that will be winners in a commercial market competition, is always seductive, but the evidence, from our studies and others, suggests that such strategy is to be avoided.

Notes

1. R. R. Nelson, Ed., Government and Technical Change: A Cross-Industry Analysis (Pergamon, New York, 1982). The authors responsible for the industry studies are: agriculture, Robert Evenson, Yale University; automobiles, Lawrence J. White, New York University; computers, Barbara Katz, New York University, and Almarin Phillips, University of Pennsylvania; housing, John Quigley, University of California, Berkeley; pharmaceuticals, Henry Grabowski and John Vernon, Duke University; and semiconductors, Richard Levin, Yale University. The study was supported by grant NSG7636 from the National Aeronautics and Space Administration.

2. Each author (or pair of authors) was responsible for an individual chapter, but the group agreed on a common format for the cases, and it met several times (sometimes with other scholars and representatives from government and industry) to discuss and integrate the chapters. R. Nelson was responsible for a synthetic "cross-cutting" chapter, which was in turn discussed and commented upon by the group.

3. The most influential of these models was by Kenneth Arrow [K. Arrow: "The allocation of resources to invention," in The Rate and Direction of Inventive Activity: Economic and Social Factors, R. R. Nelson, Ed. (Princeton University Press, Princeton, N.J., 1962)]. But see also H. Demsetz, "Information and efficiency: Another view," J. Law Econ. 12, 1, (1969).

4. K. Arrow and R. Lind, "Uncertainty and the evaluation of public investment," American Economic Review 60 (No. 3), 364, 1970.

5. The notion that "competitive"—that is, atomistic—firms innovate less than larger, "oligopolistic" firms has been called the Schumpeterian hypothesis, since those who read the work of Joseph Schumpeter through a certain set of spectacles discerned an argument of this sort in his Capitalism, Socialism, and Democracy (Harper, New York, 1942). The argument was stripped down to a more elemental form and popularized by John Kenneth Galbraith, especially in his The New Industrial State (Houghton-Mifflin, Boston, 1967).

6. Organization for Economic Cooperation and Development, Technical Change and Economic Progress (Organization for Economic Cooperation and Development, Paris, 1980). It may be significant that both the United States and Britain devoted an unusually high

fraction of R&D to defense. But even when differences in defense R&D spending are accounted for, intercountry differentials in productivity growth seem better correlated with such matters as physical investment than with overall R&D spending.

7. N. Rosenberg, "U.S. technological leadership and foreign competition: 'De te fabula narratur?'" (photocopy, Stanford University, November 1981).

8. R. R. Nelson and S. Winter, "In search of a useful theory of innovation," Res. Policy 6, 36 (1977).

9. R. R. Nelson, "Research on productivity growth and productivity differences: Dead ends and new departures," J. Econ. Lit. 19, 1029 (1981).

10. See generally K. Pavitt and W. Walker, "Government policies toward industrial innovation: A review," Res. Policy 5 (No. 1) (1976).

From Science, February 18, 1984. Reprinted by permission of the American Association For the Advancement of Science, 1515 Massachusetts Avenue, N.W., Washington, D.C.

CHAPTER THREE:
CHANGING ECONOMIC STRUCTURE

Overview

Lynn Martin

The pace of global economic change is quickening. U.S. industry, once unchallenged in world markets, is now facing foreign competition in both the domestic and global markets. This has led some observers to conclude that without a comprehensive infusion of Federal Government energy, these industries will collapse like a black hole and drag all concerns directly and indirectly related to them down the vortex.

Proponents of industrial policy assume that America is "deindustrializing" and will continue to do so; that is, American manufacturing employment will soon become a far less significant portion of the total domestic employment picture. But, during the 1970s, the U.S. was only one of three major industrial powers—the others being Italy and Canada—to register an increase in manufacturing employment. Production grew at a faster rate than the European average during the decade, indeed at a higher rate than West Germany's. In fact, during this period, high-technology exports grew by over 200 percent.

All of this does not deny the fact that changes have occurred and are occurring in the U.S. economy. Yet, we should understand what these changes are, and correct only that which needs correcting. In short, we must avoid policies which, in the words of Brookings Institution senior fellow Robert Z. Lawrence, "will delay adjustment" and produce "strictures on mobility [that] are likely to retard adaptation."

In his article, Lawrence argues that "the United States has not been undergoing deindustrialization," and that "the net impact of international competition on the overall size of the U.S. manufacturing sector has been small and positive." To support these contentions Lawrence examines data on employment, capital formation, R&D, and productivity, and notes, for example: "the United States increased its employment in manufacturing more rapidly than any other major industrial country, including Japan."

While Lawrence denies that the U.S. is deindustrializing, he does not deny that resources need to be shifted to high-growth areas. Where he seems to part company with industrial policy proponents is in his concern with the potential loss of adaptability that could result from the implementation of industrial policy. As he concludes: "If changes in industrial policy are adopted, they should be made on the grounds that they improve productivity and stimulate economic growth. They should not be undertaken because of fears, based largely on confusion about the sources of economic change..."

Lawrence's major concern is further highlighted by Princeton University economics professor William H. Branson. According to Branson, "the data on the changes in the composition of U.S. trade since World War II... show a flexible economy that is moving labor and capital resources into sectors where the U.S. performs best..." He then goes on to say: "Rather than an industrial policy aimed at supporting declining industries or subsidizing already profitable ones, we need an adjustments policy that minimizes the cost of flexibility." He includes plant closings, worker displacement, equipment obsolescence, and demographic shifting among the costs of a flexible economy.

In examining our economic structure, Branson points out that "the high-skill, high-techonology basis for our comparative advantage in trade was well established before World War II." As a result, when the oil price shocks of the 1970s occurred, the U.S. was able to draw upon its comparative advantage in specific areas, and increase exports dramatically to offset our increased costs from imported oil. This leads him to conclude: "The growth in U.S. exports is the real economic news of the 1970s."

Branson then goes on to discuss how the U.S. can retain a "relative" or "comparative" advantage as the global economic structure evolves. He argues that "a macroeconomic policy that permits realistic levels of U.S. exchange rates and interest rates is essential if our 'high-tech' industries are to be competitive and continue to grow." He also points out that our ability to adjust to a changing economy depends upon our ability to resist pressures to preserve the industrial status quo. As a result, he favors, for example, a worker retraining program which he believes would help workers adjust to rather than resist economic change.

The third article in this chapter, by Pat Choate of TRW, is particularly interesting because of the author's evolution from industrial policy supporter to industrial policy critic. Choate holds that "U.S. industry must concentrate on the basics—cost, quality, service, and innovation," rather than relying on federal subsidies or "bailouts." Like Branson and Lawrence, he also does not posit the demise of U.S. manufacturing.

Choate contends that with proper adaptation to shifting market forces, U.S. "manufacturing will continue to be a major source of good jobs well into the foreseeable future." But Choate also recognizes that government, like it or not, does play a role in U.S. industrial competitiveness. To Choate, "the issue is not one of whether government will be involved, but one of how and how much." In this regard, Choate is critical of many current government interventions, which he believes have slowed productivity growth rates, reduced the U.S. share of world exports for services and for high-technology products, and generally contributed to a dulling of the U.S. economy's competitive edge. Included among these interventions are anti-trust policy and regulatory rules.

In place of an industrial policy that picks "winners" and "losers," Choate believes that the U.S. will successfully adapt to economic change if it better manages its current array of microeconomic interventions. For example, he points out that the federal government annually spends $30 billion on public works investments, but does not have any long-term capital investment strategy. The result too often is pork barrel spending.

Lawrence, Branson, and Choate agree that industrial policy proposals are largely knee-jerk reactions to inaccurate reports of a decline in U.S. industrial competitiveness. They also agree that America IS industrially competitive, she has enormous human and capital resources, and IS capable, with limited federal macro and micro economic lubrication, of maintaining a sufficient degree of flexibility and adaptability in contending with a changing global and domestic economic structure.

The Myth of U.S. Deindustrialization

Robert Z. Lawrence

For the first time since World War II, employment in U.S. manufacturing has fallen for three consecutive years. The 10.4 percent decline from 1979 to 1982 is the largest since the wartime economy was demobilized. The current slump is also unusual because international trade has made an important contribution: normally, the volume of manufactured goods imports falls steeply in a recession—yet from 1980 to 1982, it rose by 8.3 percent. Normally, U.S. manufactured exports reflect growth in export markets abroad—yet despite a 5.3 percent rise in these markets from 1980 to 1982, the volume of U.S. manufactured exports dropped 17.5 percent.

Are these developments the predictable consequences of three years of demand restraint and a strong dollar, or do they result from deep-rooted structural changes?

There are widely held views that the recession has simply dramatized a secular decline in the U.S. industrial base. One of these views blames U.S. producers for the trend: Americans fail to produce quality goods because managers are myopic and care only about short-term profits, workers lack discipline and are shackled by work rules, and labor and management look on one another as adversaries. Others blame the U.S. government. On the one hand, there are those who fault it for excessive interference—for restrictive regulatory practices that have raised production costs; for faulty tax rules which have discouraged investment, savings, and innovation; and for trade protection that has slowed adjustment to to international competition. On the other hand there are those who blame government neglect. The United States, they contend, has failed to plan and coordinate its industrial evoluton; it ought to have policies to promote industries with potential and to assist those in decline. Finally, there is also the more fatalistic view of the decline in U.S. manufacturing as the inevitable result of rapid international diffusion of U.S. technology.

While some argue that particular deficiencies have become worse over time, others point to changes in the environment that have made U.S. structural flaws increasingly costly. As long as competition was primarily domestic, it is argued, weaknesses were obscured. But as global trade expanded, U.S. firms were forced to meet foreign competitors staffed with superior work forces and managers and backed by superior government policies.

FOUR UNFOUNDED ASSUMPTIONS

The perceived effect of international competition has grown to the point that it is frequently cited as the major source of structural change in the U.S. economy and the primary reason for the declining share of manufacturing in U.S. employment. This change is viewed with some alarm, both because manufacturing activity is considered intrinsically desirable and because of the adjustment costs associated with the shift. In addition, some argue that this decline in U.S. comparative advantage does not result from an inevitable process of technological diffusion or from changes in factors of production, but from the industrial and trade policies adopted by other nations. Without similar policies, some contend that the United States will eventually become an economy specialized in farm products and services--"a nation of hamburger stands."

Yet, while the role of the deficiencies in U.S. policies and practices in retarding productivity growth over the past decade remains unresolved, the links between these deficiencies, trade performance, and shifts in economic structure have not been convincingly demonstrated. There are several implicit assumptions in the current discussion about U.S. industrial performance that I will show to be inappropriate. First, the policy discussion often presumes that rapid productivity growth will increase the share of resources devoted to an activity, that "higher productivity will create jobs." It implicitly assumes the existence of elastic demand. As the experience of U.S. agriculture has demonstrated, however, rapid productivity growth in the face of limited markets may have the opposite effect. Indeed, the declining employment in Japanese manufacturing in the 1970s and the contrasting rise in U.S. employment suggest that manufacturing productivity may be NEGATIVELY associated with employment.

Second, the discussion presumes that a decline in international technological lead in a particular area will reduce the resources devoted to that activity. It assumes implicitly that an erosion in absolute advantage will lead to an erosion in COMPARATIVE advantage. Yet, even though foreign productive capacities are converging to those of the United States, the U.S. COMPARATIVE advantage in high-technology products has actually increased.

Third, the discussion implicitly presumes that the trade balance can decline indefinitely. It ignores the automatic adjustment mechanisms that tend to keep the trade balance in goods and services within fairly narrow bounds. An increase in imports eventually leads to an increase in exports. When global demand shifts away from U.S. products, it creates an excess supply of American goods and an excess demand for foreign goods. Since the relative price of U.S. goods may have to fall to restore the trade balance, this will INCREASE the resources devoted to export production, for a decline in the terms of trade entails providing more exports for any given volume of imports. Indeed, the decline in U.S. terms of trade associated with the real devaluations of the dollar between 1973 and 1980 contributed to the rise in U.S. employment due to trade over that period.

Fourth, international trade is neither the only nor the most important source of structural change. In many cases, trade has simply reinforced the effects of demand and technological change. At least five factors have had important effects on the U.S. industrial base.

o The share of manufactured products in consumer spending has declined secularly because of the pattern of demand associated with rising U.S. income levels.

o Some of the long-run decline in the share of manufacturing in total employment reflects the relatively more rapid productivity growth in this sector.

o Because the demand for manufactured goods is highly sensitive to the overall growth rate of GNP, manufacturing production has been slowed disproportionately by the sluggish overall growth in the global economy since 1973.

o Shifts in the pattern of U.S. international specialization have arisen from changes in comparative advantage; these, in turn, result from changes in relative factor endowments and production capabilities associated with foreign economic growth and policies.

o Short-run changes in U.S. international competitiveness have come from changes in exchange rates and cyclical conditions both at home and abroad.

The appropriate choice of policy hinges on the relative impacts of these various factors on current U.S. industrial performance. Given the radical changes in the world economy after 1973, the period from 1973 to 1980 is the most relevant sample for current policy discussions. The data for this period show stagnation, volatile exchange rates, and increasing government intervention in trade; and it is during these years, it is alleged, that foreign industrial policies damaged the U.S. manufacturing base. The data also allow comparison of U.S. industrial performance with those of other major industrial countries in a period when comparative performance is less heavily influenced by relative stages of development.

Observations for 1973 to 1980, however, may be unduly influenced by the different cyclical positions prevailing in the end-point years. Because capacity utilization in manufacturing was similar in 1970 and 1980, U.S. data for the entire decade are used to provide a second, cyclically neutral, measure of structural changes. Observations for 1970-1980 are still influenced by changes in the real exchange rate of the dollar in these years. As measured by the International Monetary Fund, relative U.S. export prices for manufactured goods were 13.5 percent lower in 1980 than in 1970. In evaluating the results, therefore, it should be kept in mind that the U.S. trade performance during the 1970s depended in part upon this price-adjustment process.

DEFINING DEINDUSTRIALIZATION

The contention that declining U.S. international competitiveness has induced the country's deindustrialization is wrong on two counts. First, in the most relevant sense, the United States has not been undergoing deindustrialization. Second, over the period 1973 to 1980, the net impact of international competition on the overall size of the U.S. manufacturing sector has been small and positive.

The term "deindustrialization" needs further elaboration. What is industry? Does it, for example, include the construction and mining sectors or refer more narrowly, as we will interpret it here (partly for reasons of data availability), to the manufacturing sector alone? Does "deindustrialization" refer to a drop in the OUTPUT of industry, or to the INPUTS (e.g., capital and/or labor) devoted to industry? Does it refer to an ABSOLUTE decline in the volume of output from (or inputs to) manufacturing, or simply a RELATIVE decline in the growth of manufacturing outputs (inputs) as compared to output (inputs) in the rest of the economy?

Since industrial policy is generally concerned with easing adjustment, absolute deindustrialization with respect to factors of production would probably be the definition that fits current policy concerns about the manufacturing sector. While a declining SHARE of output or employment could change the relative power of industrial workers or the character of a society, an absolute decline in industrial employment means much greater problems of adjustment.

This distinction is relevant: measured by the size of its manufacturing labor force, capital stock, and output growth, the United States has not experienced absolute deindustrialization over either the period 1950-1973 or 1973-1980. Employment in U.S. manufacturing rose from 15.24 million in 1950 to 16.8 million in 1960, 19.4 million in 1970, 20.1 million in 1973, and 20.3 million in 1980. The capital stock in manufacturing grew at an annual rate of 3.3 percent from 1960 to 1973, and 4.5 percent between 1973 and 1980. Output in manufacturing increased at a 3.9 percent annual rate between 1960 and 1973 and a 1.1 percent annual rate from 1978 to 1980.

Judged by the output share of goods, the United States was no more a service economy in 1980 than it was in 1960. In 1960, 1973, and 1980 the ratio of goods output to GNP (measured in 1972 dollars) was 45.6, 45.6, and 45.3 percent, respectively. Similarly, the ratio of value added in manufacturing to GNP (in 1972 dollars) was actually somewhat higher in 1973 than it was in 1950. Nonetheless, from 1950 to 1973, the SHARES of expenditure, employment, capital stock, and R&D devoted to the manufacturing sector declined. Factors on both the demand and supply sides account for this. As U.S. incomes have risen, Americans have allocated increasing shares of their budgets to items in the service sector such as government services, education, medical care, finance, and real estate services. At the same time, productivity in manufacturing has increased more rapidly than elsewhere in the economy. Although the more rapid growth in manufacturing productivity has led to slower increases in manufacturing prices, the demand stimulated by the relative price decline for manufactured goods has not offset the fall in the share of resources devoted to value added in manufacturing. As a result, overall real industrial output has risen about as rapidly as GNP, but the shares of employment and capital in manufactured goods have declined.

From 1973 to 1982 there has been a marked acceleration in the rate at which manufacturing's share of output and employment has fallen. But this should have been expected, given the slow overall growth in GNP and the fact that growth in labor productivity (output per man-hour) fell less in manufacturing than in the rest of the economy. The demand for manufacturing output is particularly sensitive to fluctuations in income. The demand for goods, particularly durables, is inherently more sensitive to short-run income fluctuations than the demand for services, because many such purchases can be easily postponed. Thus the generally slow growth in U.S. GNP from 1973 to 1980 was reflected in disproportionately slow growth in the manufacturing sector.

The relationship between the growth of manufacturing and the overall growth of the economy can be summarized quite well by using standard econometric analysis. The results show that industrial performance is a magnification of performance in the overall economy: if GNP grows at 1.7 percent per year, there will be no increase in manufacturing production. But for each percentage point increase (decrease) of GNP growth above 1.7 percent, manufacturing output will rise (fall) by 2.2 percentage points. The analysis shows that, based on the estimates from 1960 to 1973, one can forecast industrial production for the period 1978 to 1982, taking actual GNP as given, with remarkable accuracy. Thus, there is no puzzle in explaining aggregate manufacturing production. It is almost exactly what one should have expected given the performance of the total economy.

EMPLOYMENT, PLANT, R&D

While the overall level of manufacturing output has matched its historic relationship with GNP, the relationship between the growth of outputs and inputs has changed. As a result of the decline in productivity growth in manufacturing since 1978, given rates of output growth are now associated with somewhat higher rates of employment and capital growth. Analysis indicates that, taking manufacturing output as given, manufacturing employment growth has been about 1.36 percent per year higher than it would have been without the decline in manufacturing productivity growth. Thus employment has actually held up better than might have been anticipated from past relationships.

Probably the most commonly provided reason for poor U.S manufacturing performance is the failure of businesses to invest in new plant and equipment. Yet, while there has been a marked decline in the growth of the capital-labor ratio in the economy overall since 1973, the measured growth of the net capital stock in manufacturing has been remarkably rapid. Although the ratio of the net capital stock to full-time equivalent employees in manufacturing grew at about 2.03 percent per year from 1950 to 1973, it grew at 3.8 percent per year from 1974 to 1980. This supports the view that automation has actually accelerated. And, while historically the ratio of the net capital stock in U.S. manufacturing to the net stock in the rest of the economy declined (from 0.30 in the 1950s to 0.26 in the 1960s to 0.237 in 1973), since 1973 the capital stock in manufacturing has actually grown more rapidly than in the rest of the private economy.

The 1970s saw a much-publicized decline in the growth of real R&D expenditures. While real R&D spending increased 3.1 percent per year from 1960 to 1973, it fell to a 2.5 percent annual growth rate from 1973 to 1980. But this does not reflect a similar drop in real R&D spending in U.S. industry. Between 1960 and 1972, such spending in manufacturing grew 1.9 percent per year. From 1972 to 1979 (the latest data available), it accelerated to 2.4 percent. A similar pattern is evident in industry hiring. While the number of scientists and engineers employed in industry R&D grew at 1.6 percent between 1960 and 1973, growth from 1973 to 1980 averaged 3.2 percent per year.

The increased commitment of plant, equipment, and R&D expenditures makes the decline in productivity growth in U.S. manufacturing since 1973 particularly puzzling. One question is whether the capital stock is accurately measured. Mismeasurement could be due to an increase in capital and R&D devoted to meeting regulatory requirements such as safety and pollution control, which do not show up as output. Subtracting Commerce Department estimates of the net capital stock devoted to reducing air and water pollution from the net capital stock in manufacturing lowers the growth in manufacturing capital from 4.5 to 4.2 percent per year. A second reason might be the premature retirement of capital that has become economically obsolete in changed economic conditions.

Nonetheless, as these data make clear, there has been no erosion in the U.S. industrial base. The decline in employment shares has been the predictable result of slow demand and relatively more rapid labor productivity growth in manufacturing because of an acceleration in capital formation. Paradoxically, the slow (absolute) growth in productivity has required unpredictably large increases in employment, plant and equipment, and R&D.

THE GLOBAL PERSPECTIVE

Proponents of a radical change in U.S. industrial policies contrast the ad hoc and laissez-faire policies of the United States with the systematic and interventionist practices abroad. While conceding there are marked differences in the degree to which foreign practices have succeeded, they argue that the conscious policy of managing the decline of older industries and the rise of new industries has been superior to the U.S. approach marked by malign neglict. Similarly, the broader provision of social services in European economies, the more extensive rights to their jobs enjoyed by workers, and the greater restrictions on plant closings have all been held up as worthy of emulation. Opponents of such policies argue that they will delay adjustment, for the government is most likely to be captured by forces seeking to preserve the status quo, and strictures on mobility are likely to retard adaptation.

It is particularly important that international comparisons be made on the basis of performance since 1973, for policies that succeeded amid strong global growth and economic expansion might not be appropriate for the current era of stagnation.

The 1972-74 commodity boom and the inflation that accompanied it brought a new era. All developed countries have been plagued by low rates of investment, slow growth, and inflation. The problems associated with high inflation and energy shocks have destroyed investors' confidence. They have learned from their experiences in 1974 (and again in 1979) that a political disruption in the Middle East or a sudden increase in domestic inflation may at any time force their governments to adopt policies that bring on a recession leaving them with excess capacity. The rate of investment has slumped, the growth of the heavy manufacturing industries has been cut, and consumption expenditures have risen as a share of GDP. Industries with long gestation periods for investment, such as steel and shipbuilding, have been particularly hard hit by the post-1973 slump. There is insufficient demand for the products of plants that were built on the basis of overoptimistic projections of market growth in the late 1960s.

By a wide variety of indicators, the relative performance of U.S. manufacturing since 1973 has improved. The declines in the growth of manufacturing production, productivity growth, employment, and investment in manufacturing were all smaller here than in other industrial nations. While U.S. growth was among the slowest prior to 1973, since that time it has been quite typical for a developed country. Although trailing Japan, U.S. industrial production grew more rapidly than in Germany, France, or the United Kingdom.

It is in Europe rather than in the United States that employment is undergoing absolute deindustrialization. Compared with historical trends, industrial production in Japan was abnormally strong while industrial production in Europe is unusually weak. Econometric analysis relating industrial production to GNP in European countries from 1960 to 1973 demonstrates a substantial overprediction of the level of industrial production in 1980. In the case of Japan, the analysis underpredicts industrial production (by 12 percent in 1980).

According to disaggregated statistics for industry (OECD INDUSTRIAL PRODUCTION, various issues) U.S. output growth from 1973 to 1980 for food, textiles, apparel, chemicals, glass, and fabricated metals products was more rapid than that of either Germany or Japan. Primary metals were an exception. Although U.S. growth lagged behind Japan in the various engineering categories, it trailed German growth only in basic metals production and transportation equipment.

A closer look at several important measures of industrial vitality gives a similar picture of the supposed American deindustrialization.

Employment. The employment record of the U.S. manufacturing sector may come as a surprise to those concerned about deindustrialization: from 1973 to 1980, the United States increased its employment in manufacturing more rapidly than any other major industrial country, including Japan. Moreover, since the average workweek declined more rapidly abroad, the relatively larger growth in U.S. manufacturing employment is even more conspicious. A comparison between the United States and Japan indicates that Japanese employment in sectors such as transportation, electrical machinery, nonelectrical machinery, chemicals, and nonferrous metals grew less rapidly or declined more than that in the United States.

As the case of Japan makes clear, in the current global environment of relatively slow growth in demand, rapid increases in productivity do not necessarily increase employment. Indeed, compared with the United States, the faster increases in Japanese productivity have entailed the more rapid process of labor-force deindustrialization. In the case of Europe, employment opportunities in manufacturing have decreased because faster productivity growth has been combined with relatively slower growth in output.

Capital formation. If we compare gross fixed investment in manufacturing in the United States with that of industrialized European countries, the sluggish growth of such investment in Europe is apparent; only in France was it above its 1970 levels in 1979. Compare the ratios of European investment in manufacturing with overall gross fixed investment in those countries: in contrast to the United States, most of the European economies are allocating proportionately less of their new capital formation to industrial production than they did in 1970.

Just as an automobile may be decelerating and yet going faster than another, so one country may have a declining growth rate for investment with a capital stock growing at a relatively faster rate. Thus capital stock measures are required. Such estimates are gathered by the United Nations. They indicate that in contrast to its previous performance, the U.S. capital stock in manufacturing grew as rapidly as those in Europe.

Research and Development. Since 1972, the United States has maintained its share in R&D spending among industrial countries, thereby reversing the relative decline of the late 1960s and early 1970s, when U.S. government-funded R&D was cut back while R&D spending in other major countries advanced rapidly. From 1972 to 1980, the growth in business-funded R&D in the United States has been similar to the growth in France, Germany, and Japan; and while government-funded R&D in the United States has not grown at the Japanese pace, it has exceeded the rise in support provided by the governments of France, Germany, and the United Kingdom.

According to OECD estimates, by a wide variety of indicators, the United States continues to dominate other industrial countries in its commitment to R&D. In 1977, for example, spending on R&D in U.S. manufacturing was equal to about 6.5 percent of the domestic U.S. industrial output. By contrast, spending on manufacturing R&D in Japan, the United Kingdom, and Germany amounted to 3.7, 5.0, and 4.0 percent, respectively, of industrial output. Indeed, PRIVATELY FUNDED American R&D alone was equal to 4.4 percent of manufacturing product. In absolute terms in 1979, measured at purchasing power parity levels, the United States spent about 1.5 times as much as Japan, Germany, France, and the United Kingdom combined and employed about 1.3 times as many scientists and engineers. By contrast, manufacturing employment in these countries in 1979 was 1.5 times that in the United States. The OECD has also ranked industrial countries according to the percentage of manufacturing output spent on R&D in a variety of industry groups during the 1970s. The United States ranked first in manufacturing overall and in the electrical, aerospace, machinery, and transportation categories.

Productivity. Measured both in terms of the ratio of total output to all inputs and in output per man-hour, U.S. productivity growth in manufacturing, as in the economy as a whole, has slowed down in the period since 1973. Over the same period, however, there has been an even larger slowdown in foreign productivity growth, both in manufacturing and in the whole economy. Careful studies have been unable to provide convincing explanations for these slowdowns, and I will not attempt an investigation here. It should, however, be noted that despite some convergence since 1973, the U.S. productivity growth rate in manufacturing remains the slowest of any major industrial country.

Measured by output per man-hour, however, the United States continues to be the world's most productive manufacturing nation. According to A.D. Roy, for example, output per employed worker-year in U.S. manufacturing in 1980 was about 16 percent higher than in Japan, 21.7 percent higher than in Germany, and 31.3 percent higher than in France. To be sure, America no longer leads in all industries. According to the 1981 White Paper on International Trade issued by the government of Japan, Japanese productivity levels in 1979 were above those of the United States in steel (108 percent above U.S. levels), general machinery (11 percent higher), electrical machinery (19 percent), transportation equipment (24 percent), and precision machinery and equipment (34 percent).

Some economists have unfavorably contrasted the U.S. failure to promote industrial adjustment with the explicit adjustment policies followed in Europe and Japan. It is therefore of some interest to compare the shifts in the U.S. industrial structure with those in other major economies to determine whether in fact U.S. industrial adaptation has been lagging. To explore this question I have used the matched set of data collected by the United Nations. These provide fairly disaggregated information on industries at the three-digit ISIC level.[1] First, I selected the group of industries that is generally considered to have high growth potential. They are characterized by relative intensity in R&D and by rapid rates of technological innovation. The sample includes chemicals, plastic products, machinery, and professional instruments and typically provides up to about 35 percent of manufacturing employment in major industrial nations. Next, I calculated the share of total manufacturing employment these industries accounted for in the United States, Germany, and Japan and compared growth in these shares between 1973 and 1979.

Although employment shares in all three countries increased, the 8.9 percent rise in the U.S. share far exceeded those of both Japan (up 0.6 percent) and Germany (up 3.0 percent). A similar analysis was performed for a group of slow growers—labor-intensive industries such as textiles, apparel, leather, footwear, and furniture, and capital-intensive industries such as metals, metal products, and shipbuilding. This group also typically accounted for between 30 and 35 percent of total employment. In this case, Germany had the most rapid decline in the share of employment (9.2 percent), while Japan and the U.S. had shifts quite similar in magnitude. While the United States moved out of labor-intensive industries faster than Japan, the drop in the Japanese share of the capital-intensive group exceeded that of the United States.

These results should, of course, be treated with some caution because of the relatively aggregative nature of the industry divisions and the possible discrepancies in national classification schemes. Nonetheless, they contradict assertions of America's relative failure to shift resources toward high-growth sectors. They indicate that the United States has been about as successful as Japan in reducing the role of the low-growth group.

THE EUROPEAN DILEMMA

I have pointed to the marked contrast in European economic performance before and after 1973, a contrast that is particularly evident in data on industrial performance. European manufacturing production has declined by more than might have been expected, given GNP. Employment has fallen and productivity growth slowed. While Germany has been relatively successful in shifting out of slow-growth industries, it has been less successful in moving into new ones.

European governments have assumed much greater responsibility than those in Japan or the United States for providing steady increases in standards of living, and a much greater degree of job tenure is provided in Europe than is common in the United States. In the 1950s and 1960s these guarantees were relatively costless, for rapid growth in demand facilitated job retention, while rising productivity growth made higher wages affordable. With the shocks and slow growth in the 1970s, however, governments were forced to make good on the guarantees. Partly because they were backstopped by generous social payments by schemes such as indexation, growth in European real wages exceeded the pace warranted by changes in productivity and the terms of trade. This squeezed profits, discouraged investment, and slowed growth. While manufacturing employment declined, the service sectors in Europe were unable to provide employment for new labor force entrants and those displaced from manufacturing. By contrast, the slowdown in the growth of U.S. manufacturing employment opportunities was more than matched by the expansion in services.

Whereas European unemployment rates have been considerably lower than those in the United States for most of the period since World War II, by 1982 the average unemployment rates in the United States and the European commmunity were 9.7 and 9.5 percent, respectively. Structural unemployment, however, seems much higher in Europe. According to the OECD, in the United States in 1982 about 16.6 percent of the unemployed had been without a job for more than six months. By contrast, in Germany, France, and the United Kingdom, the long-term unemployed were 38.1, 55.8, and 45.7 percent, respectively, of the total unemployed. In 1979, males over the age of 45 constituted 36 percent of all unemployed German males, whereas in the United States, older males were 17 percent of the unemployed. Similarly, older women were 29 percent of the unemployed in Germany, and 15 percent of those in the United States.

THE IMPORTANCE OF RELATIVE PRICES

Compared with its postwar track record, since 1973 the U.S. manufacturing sector has fared relatively well in comparison with other industrial countries. This might have been expected, given the relative exhaustion of catch-up gains which others could enjoy by adopting U.S. techniques. The U.S. performance may also be ascribed to its greater flexibility in a period marked by external shocks. In particular, U.S. real wage growth has been more adaptable and U.S. labor more mobile. The American share of manufacturing employment in high growth industries has increased more rapidly than that of Germany or Japan. There are, therefore, strengths as well as weaknesses in the U.S. industrial system.

Flexible exchange rates have been important to U.S. trade performance. From 1973 to 1980, partly because of the real devaluation of the dollar, foreign trade provided a net addition to output and jobs in U.S. manufacturing. From 1980 to 1982, the erosion in relative price competitiveness has been the source of the declines in employment due to manufactured goods trade. Changes in the real exchange rate are effective in moving the current account toward equilibrium determined by expenditure patterns. In 1970 and 1980, the current account was a similar percentage of GNP. This stability was achieved in part by growth in the manufactured goods trade balance because of real devaluation. In the 1980s, the shift toward large full-employment government deficits unmatched by lower private absorption entails a current account deficit as foreign savings help finance the government deficit. This is accomplished in part by a manufactured goods trade deficit achieved through real appreciation. If these trade deficits are viewed as undesirable, policies to lower full-employment government deficits should be considered.

The decline in the manufactured goods trade balance over the past two years is not the result of a sudden erosion in U.S. international competitiveness brought about by foreign industrial and trade policies. It is predictable, given previous trends and current levels of economic activity and relative prices. Given a continuation of trends in U.S. and foreign trade policies and growth patterns, in the absence of relative price changes, the U.S. trade balance in manufactured goods would register small annual declines. If required for overall external equilibrium, these declines could be offset by minor improvements in relative U.S. prices.

There has not been increased turbulence in the demand for industrial workers across manufacturing industries. The recent rise in dislocation is principally related to the slow overall growth in employment rather than an increase in structural change at any given growth rate.

The perceptions of an absolute decline in the U.S. industrial base and the belief that foreign competition has made a major contribution to that decline stem from the reinforcing effects of U.S. trade and domestic growth and the nature of adjustment difficulties associated with declines in industries adversely affected. The troubled industries are large and highly unionized, and the average plant size is large. Workers displaced from several of these industries face the prospect of considerably lower wages.

The U.S. comparative advantage in unskilled labor and standardized capital intensive products has been declining secularly. And because of slow domestic economic growth, the home market for these products has not expanded rapidly. But the U.S. comparative advantage in high-technology products has strengthened while the demand for high-technology products has grown relatively more rapidly in a climate of stagnation. In general, however, structural changes in the U.S. economy during this period arose mainly from domestic factors.

Let me offer an overall conclusion based upon this evidence. If changes in industrial policy are adopted, they should be made on the grounds that they improve productivity and stimulate economic growth. They should not be undertaken because of fears, based largely on confusion about the sources of economic change, that policies that appear inadvisable on domestic grounds are required in order to compete internationally.

1. Editor's Note: The ISIC (International Standard Industrial Classification) is a code used by both business and government to classify various industrial sectors.

Reprinted by permission of M.E. Sharpe, Inc., 80 Business Park Drive, Armonk, New York, from Challenge, November/December 1983.

The Myth of Deindustrialization

William Branson

Discussion of industrial policy is heard everywhere in Washington today, as political campaigners gear up for 1984. Deindustrialization theorists present an image of an American economy so muscle-bound that it cannot cope with instability and structural change in the world economy and is inevitably losing its presence in basic industries. For some unknown reason, McDonald's ubiquitous hamburgers are a favorite illustration of the problem. A May issue of Time magazine, for example, quotes the chairman of Firestone Tire and Rubber as saying, "It is utter nonsense that we are going to become a high-tech and service economy. The high-tech companies have more manufacturing offshore than here. The idea that we can have an economy by selling hamburgers to each other is absurd." Hamburgers aside, the comment reflects the widely felt fear that basic industries will "disappear" due to foreign competition, leaving the United States with no manufacturing capacity or jobs. To survive, it is argued, the economy needs an industrial policy, as well as some sort of protection against outside shocks.

The data on the changes in the composition of U.S trade since World War II, however, tell just the opposite story. They show a flexible economy that is moving labor and capital resources into sectors where the U.S. performs best in a world of increasing economic integration and competitive pressure.

This flexibility has costs, which are emphasized by the deindustrialization theorists. Plants close or move, labor requires retraining, equipment becomes obsolete, towns and cities shrink or grow. The declining industries lobby Congress for protection and try to convince the public that the United State is losing out in international trade. But the movement of resources away from declining, low-productivity industries is a movement toward high-productivity areas of expansion. The flexibility of our economy permits, even encourages, adjustment to the changing world economy and the changing U.S. position in it. Rather than an industrial policy aimed at supporting declining industries or subsidizing already profitable ones, we need an adjustment policy that minimizes the costs of flexibility.

Since World War II, U.S. trade has gone through two major adjustment periods. First came the erosion in our temporary postwar position of being net exporters of nearly everything. As the economies of Europe, Japan, and the newly industrializing countries gained strength, U.S. trade moved back to its pre-war pattern. The second adjustment followed the oil price increases of 1973-74--which raised our net oil import bill by $65 billion between 1973 and 1981. The changes that enabled us to pay that bill were dramatic. Our trade surplus in capital goods alone, for example, rose by $32 billion.

The economic strength that those adjustments reflect is based on a productive agricultural sector and on an educated and flexible labor force. Growth in manufacturing exports comes in sectors that use intensively the skills embodied in the labor force, while imports squeeze industries that are older, more capital-intensive, and based on routine operations. As industries such as autos, textiles, and steel became internationalized during the seventies, the U.S. retained its comparative advantage in the high-skill, high-technology ends of those industries, and lost only the lower-skill manufactures to the developing countries.

Since 1981, high real interest rates and an overvalued dollar have temporarily (it is to be hoped) halted this successful process of structural adjustment in the U.S. economy. They have produced a double depressing effect on the industries that manufacture durable, tradeable goods: autos, steel, equipment. This, in turn, has added to pressures for industrial policy or for protection--because a MACROECONOMIC problem is misdiagnosed as a trade problem. The basic problem in these industries since 1981 has been caused by fiscal and monetary policy, and will not be rectified by trade or adjustment policies.

A POCKET HISTORY OF U.S. POSTWAR TRADE

During the years just after World War II, the United States was a net exporter of all kinds of manufactures that it would normally import. This artificial situation could not last.

The broad outlines of the "normal" position can be seen as early as 1930. The United States was a major net exporter of fuel, capital goods, and autos--the latter two being the high-technology industries of the time--and an importer of consumer goods and industrial inputs other than fuel and chemicals. Trade in agricultural goods was roughly balanced, and the chemical and arms industries were just developing. This pattern held even after the full force of the Great Depression hit the U.S. economy in the 1930s, with two exceptions. The midwestern drought and depopulation led to large imports and trade deficits in agriculture from 1935 to 1939, and the growing chemical industry was providing a rapidly increasing surplus. These trends are reflected in the 1937 trade figures. The high-skill, high-technology basis for our comparative advantage in trade was well established before World

War II.

The 1947 data show clearly the effect of World War II. The United States had substantial surpluses in all categories that year, including nearly $1 billion in each of its traditional import fields of consumer goods and other industrial materials. And the overall trade surplus reached a post-war peak of $9.5 billion, compared with $0.3 billion in 1937. In those years, we were, indeed, a supplier of all goods to the world. This sudden expansion in world demand for American manufactures gave birth to plants and industries that could not possibly survive when international competition was reestablished. It was the pressure on these noncompetitive industries during the 1950s that helped create the post-war impression that the Untied States was losing out in trade. Actually, our trade was just moving back to its pre-war basis of comparative advantage.

Comparison of the data for 1930, 1937, and 1960 is convincing on this point. In all categories except agriculture, the pattern of surpluses and deficits was the same in 1960 as in 1930 and 1937—although the surpluses and deficits were generally larger, reflecting the overall expansion of world trade. We had also become a major exporter of farm products.

During the decade of the 1960s, the dollar was increasingly overvalued, and that led to a shrinkage in the United States' shares of world manufacturing exports and in its overall trade surplus, from $5.5 billion in 1960 to $3.3 billion in 1970. This was also partly due to the overheating of the economy during the expansion phase of the Vietnam War, 1965-68. Much of the automobile industry lost its high-technology character and production became routinized. Activity moved abroad to low-wage areas—shifting U.S. trade in autos from a surplus to a deficit of $2.2 billion. In addition, as the growth in fuel demand outpaced supply and major sources were developed in the Arab world, our small fuel deficit grew to $1.4 billion. But the biggest change in trade during the decade came in capital equipment, where the surplus increased by $5.5 billion. By 1970, even with an overvalued dollar and deficits in fuel and autos, net exports in capital goods, chemicals, and military equipment were big enough to provide a trade surplus of $3.3 billion.

The pattern of trade in 1973 was much the same as in 1970. The main differences are in agriculture, where major strength was developing, and in fuel, where the deficit increased by $5 billion in response to the first signs of the collapse in the oil companies' power and the rise in OPEC's. The real devaluation of the dollar had stabilized the U.S. share of world manufactures exports.

The year 1973 marked the end of the U.S. post-war adjustment. Trade was roughly balanced. We had large and growing export surpluses in our areas of comparative advantage—agriculture, capital and military equipment, chemicals—along with corresponding deficits in lower-technology areas such as consumer goods, autos, industrial supplies, and fuel. Growth in these deficits and surpluses signaled a continuing transfer of capital and labor resources from declining low-productivity to expanding high-productivity industries. The United States was set for a resurgence of expansion after the Vietnam debacle and the devaluations of 1971-1973.

Then came the oil price shock of 1974, which set off a series of oil price increases that hiked U.S. net imports of fuel from $6.4 billion in 1973 to $71 billion in 1981. Yet, over that period, our total trade deficit increased by only $29 billion. This means that enough resources were transferred from production for domestic use to production for export to produce an additional $36 billion in net exports. The growth in U.S. exports is the real economic news of the 1970s.

Which sectors were expanding net exports to pay for the additional fuel bill, and pulling resources away from domestic consumption? Agriculture, capital goods, and chemicals led the way. Between 1973 and 1981, these three areas of U.S. comparative advantage INCREASED their net export surplus by $57 billion! The deficit sectors also showed significant increases. These increasing import deficits released resources from low-productivity sectors, freeing them to move to a higher-productivity employment.

The adjustment of the 1970s, then, had two aspects. First, there was a massive increase in exports in agriculture and relatively high-technology capital goods and chemicals, helping to pay for the rising oil bill imposed by the oil price increases. Second, there was a continuation of the 1960s trend toward specialization along lines of comparative advantage, with rising surpluses in areas of relative strength and increasing deficits in areas characterized by lower technology, low-skill requirements, and routinized operations. In short, the record shows that the U.S. economy is not a noncompetitive producer in manufactures, but rather has undergone a structural adjustment toward areas of comparative advantage. This adjustment process must be nurtured and eased by policy, not stifled by protection of low-productivity jobs.

SOURCES OF U.S. COMPARATIVE ADVANTAGE

Any voluntary trade, whether between nations or persons, is based in some way on RELATIVE, or COMPARATIVE advantage. This is so obvious at the personal level that we usually do not even notice it. In all but the most backward economies, individuals specialize in their work on what they do best and then exchange their incomes for a whole range of goods that others produce. Our sales of labor services are our exports, and our purchases of consumer goods are our imports. This specialization along lines of comparative advantage depends on kinds and amounts of education and training, personal factors like strength, speed, manual skills, our preferences for kinds of work, and luck. The point is that there is a basis for the specialization and we all gain from trade. We would all be worse off if we could not specialize in production and trade the results.

In international trade, countries also specialize in production, and then trade for the broad range of consumer and investment goods their economies require. The basis for comparative advantage is obvious in the case of some countries, especially those with heavy endowments of natural resources. The comparative advantages of Kuwait in oil, South Africa in diamonds, Chile in copper, and Brazil in coffee are pretty easy to understand. Less clear is the source of comparative advantage between the industrialized countries of Europe, Japan, North America, and the newly industrializing countries.

The very stable pattern of trade that the United States has had since the late 1960s is based on our relative advantage in land and highly trained and skilled labor. In agriculture, the two combine in an extremely productive and low-cost sector that produces an export surplus of some $25 billion a year, even in the face of highly protected agriculture in Europe and Japan. In manufacturing, the U.S. comparative advantage in a skilled, educated, and mobile labor force permits U.S. industry to concentrate on production that requires high-skill inputs and uses the latest technology. These products tend to be new and to be produced in nonroutine ways that require thought and initiative in the workplace. These are the capital goods and military equipment industries, chemicals, and the innovative and high-technology end of basic industries.

Economists combine all kinds of marketable skills that are embodied in the work force in the concept of "human capital." This is the capital accumulated through years of education, on-the-job training and experience, and embodied in the individual worker. The difference between the unskilled worker's wage of around $5 an hour and the aircraft mechanic's wage of over $20 is the return on the latter's investment in human capital.

U.S. industry increasingly concentrates on goods that intensively use human capital in production. This pulls resources—labor and "ordinary" capital—from goods that use unskilled labor more intensively in production, and the production of these goods moves to countries with a comparative surplus of literate and disciplined but unskilled labor. The unskilled labor-intensive operations tend to be repetitive, disciplined processes and production lines. They produce the U.S. imports.

The correlation of human-capital intensity in U.S. exports and unskilled labor in imports is conventional wisdom among researchers on U.S. trade. In my study with Nicholas Monoyios, human capital consistently had the highest positive correlation with net exports, and unskilled labor the highest negative correlation (Journal of

International Economics, 1977). Keith Maskus and Robert Stern studied data for each year from 1958 to 1976 and obtained the same results (Journal of International Economics, 1981). Clearly the United States should look after its trade advantage in a skilled and mobile labor force.

A trade advantage in skilled labor also shows up in the use of frontier industrial technology in our export industries. The way an industry best uses skilled labor is in producing new and developing goods or using new and evolving processes. This is the basis of the concept of the "product cycle" pioneered by Raymond Vernon. High-technology countries innovate and produce high-technology products, gradually developing export markets. When the products become standardized and production routinized, manufacture shifts to areas with lower-skilled workers and lower wages; and the products become imports for the high-technology countries, whose industries move on to new frontiers. This is the story of trade in basic U.S. industries, as told below.

The very strong correlation of U.S. exports and high technology, as well as of U.S. imports and low or routine technology, is evident. (High-technology industries are defined as those having high R&D expenditures relative to total sales and a high proportion of skilled labor in their work force; the low-technology industries have low R&D expenditures and a low proportion of skilled workers.) The difference in trade patterns is striking. U.S. low-technology products show a deficit that has been growing exponentially since the early 1960s, reaching about $35 billion in 1980. Over the same period, the U.S. high-technology EXPORT surplus grew first steadily and then explosively, climbing from $12 billion to $40 billion in the last seven years. Again the economy's adjustment to the oil price shock is apparent. U.S. exports of high-technology goods, which tend to be capital goods and chemicals, increased rapidly as the economy moved resources into these sectors.

Most of that increase after 1973 was in exports to the developing countries. The U.S. high-technology surplus with these countries increased from $6 billion in 1973 to $25 billion by 1980. Our high-tech trade with Western Europe as a whole also showed a surplus that was growing but not nearly so fast. (This slowly increasing U.S. surplus, at least until 1980, reflects the tendency for industry in Western Europe to fall behind in high-technology manufacturing.) In contrast, our high-tech trade with Germany has remained roughly balanced, while that with Japan has shown an increasing deficit since the mid-1970s.

The data signals two points. First, the developing countries are an increasingly important market for U.S. manufactured exports, probably because our advantage in the goods that are produced with skilled labor is greatest RELATIVE to these countries. Second, Japan is our major competitor. The picture is one of our competing with Japan for developing country markets in the years to come.

WILL BASIC LOW-TECHNOLOGY INDUSTRY "DISAPPEAR"?

The increasing trade deficits in the low-technology sectors mean a loss of jobs in these sectors. But the fear that whole industries will disappear stems from the misconception that these large basic industries--auto, steel, and textiles--are big homogeneous backward sectors. The truth is that they are made up of many subsectors. Some of the sectors are very high-technology and skill-intensive, and in these the United States will become more competitive and will even expand its share. Other subsectors produce standard products using standard methods and a lower level of skills, and here we will become less competitive over time. These are the shrinking subsectors of the basic industries. The U.S. steel and textile industries will not "disappear." Rather they will concentrate on the advanced end of the industry, allowing the routine and lower-skill end to move abroad.

A few details will show how this process works. The iron and steel industry trade data can be broken down into three subsectors --basic materials for iron and steel, iron and steel products except advanced manufactures, and finished metal shapes and advanced manufactures. Basic materials have high transportation costs and therefore, as would be expected, show a small trade balance. Standard products, whose production is routinized and capital-intensive, show a growing deficit as manufacturing has moved abroad. Finished products, especially advanced manufactures, have remained competitive and have turned in a small surplus since the early 1970s. Far from vanishing, the American steel industry is being transformed through trade into a relatively high-technology industry.

The same is true in textiles. This industry's trade data can be broken into two subsectors. At the low-technology, low-skill end are consumer textiles, the imported clothes and fabrics that are familiar to us all. At the high-technology end are "industrial textiles," synthetic fibers that are used as industrial inputs and that are frequently produced with highly automated, computer-controlled processing equipment. The new technology began to take hold around 1970, stimulating a wave of investment and creating for the United States a comparative advantage in this end of the industry. Since 1974 we have run a surplus in industrial textiles. Here again, trade is transforming an industry's base from low skills and routine operations to high skills and technology.

A final example is provided by the auto industry, whose death has been loudly proclaimed by so many of its own executives and union leaders. In fact, however, the auto industry has become a world industry, with worldwide rationalization of production. Assembly is done near the consuming market, with parts coming from many areas. Each country will fit into this world picture, depending on which sector it provides best. To quote from Marina Whitman, a distinguished economist and vice-president of General Motors:

> Under the "world car" concept, automobiles little differentiated in size and design among different geographic areas are assembled from parts and components that are to a large extent standardized and interchangeable. The expanded production takes advantage of economies of scale and the allocative efficiencies generated by differences in factor endowments and therefore in production costs... One of the implications of these developments for the automotive trade is that the strategy of direct exports of finished vehicles will be replaced gradually by more complex trading relationships involving vehicles and parts. [Princeton Essays in International Finance, no. 143, 1981]

In the rationalized auto industry, the United States will provide parts that require skill, innovation, and technology data. The increasing total deficit in auto trade since the 1960s is due to imports of passenger cars. But since the mid-1950s, the United States has had a surplus in trade in auto parts running at about $1-2 billion. The U.S. auto industry will probably shrink some more, but it will not disappear. It will be integrated into a world system in which the United States will maintain its competitiveness in the subsectors where it performs best.

OUR COMPETITIVE POSITION THREATENED, 1981-83

In 1981 a shadow was cast over this bright picture of competitiveness and continuing adjustment toward high-productivity sectors. The shadow was the combination of the massive multi-year tax cut and the phased increase in defense spending prescribed in the 1981 budget, and the monetary tightness needed to restrain inflation in the face of the resulting budget deficits. This raised U.S. interest rates and the value of the dollar. Indeed, the 25 percent real increase in the dollar from 1980 to 1983 gave back to the world all of the competitive gains that had been achieved from 1971 to 1980. By making U.S. manufactures that much less competitive across the board, the dollar's appreciation threatens to weaken the entire U.S. industrial structure. In a March 1983 speech, Chairman Martin Feldstein of the President's Council of Economic Advisers stated the problem clearly:

> The prospect of large future deficits in the second half of the 1980s and beyond would keep long-term interest rates high, in the next few years and thereby depress spending on investment in plant and equipment and in housing. The higher real long-term interest rate would also keep the exchange interest value of the dollar very high, thus encouraging imports and weakening the competitive position of U.S. exports in the world economy. In short, the prospect of large budget deficits would mean a very lopsided and unhealthy recovery in which several key industries fail to share in the economic recovery.

The source of the problem, of course, is the Reagan administration's own budget. There is no way that adjustment and flexibility can offset the effects of high interest rates and a highly overvalued dollar in undermining the U.S. competitive position. A macroeconomic policy that permits realistic levels of U.S. exchange rates and interest rates is essential if our "high-tech" industries are to be competitive and continue to grow.

THE MORAL OF THE STORY: ADJUSTMENT TO COMPETITION

When the economy is adjusting smoothly, jobs lost in declining industries are lost to firms, but not to workers--who move on to other jobs that are opening in expanding industries. While the movement can be painful and costly, especially if we do not have an effective policy for training and relocation, the new jobs are likely to have higher productivity and perhaps higher pay than the old jobs. Nevertheless, the old jobs are surely "lost" to the shrinking basic low-technology industries, which creates serious problems for the firms, the communities, and the unions entrenched in those industries.

With plants closing or cutting back, workers having to search for new jobs, and the local tax base contracting, it is little consolation to the particular workers, unions, and towns that growth is rapid in another industry on the other side of the country. The gains from trade and adjustment go to all the consumer/taxpayers in the country, while the losses are concentrated on the few who are in the shrinking industries. Thus, it is entirely appropriate that the federal government use general tax revenues to minimize the costs of adjustment and speed the process. By and large, the capital markets move resources in the right direction, so there is no need for an industrial policy that directs the allocation of resources. What we do need, however, is a program that provides retraining and relocation assistance for workers who have to adjust and some sort of interim support for the affected communities. Designing an effective program of this kind should be a high priority for policy makers and researchers today. For it is an essential part of a policy package to keep the U.S. economy flexible and competitive.

A policy of encouraging open trade and resource reallocation can stand only as one leg of the stool. An effective assistance policy that smooths the course of adjustment and a macroeconomic policy that ends the misalignment of the dollar are the other two legs. Without any one of the three, the gains from a competitive economy will be lost.

From Regulation, AEI Journal on Government and Society, September-October 1983. Reprinted by permission of the American Enterprise Institute, Washington, D.C.

Manufacturing: Meeting the Global Competition

Pat Choate

Mark Twain once had the opportunity to refute his obituary. Basic American manufacturing now has the same chance.

Indeed, American manufacturing is far from extinct. Neither is it irrelevant to our economy. Today, American manufacturing provides employment for one in five U.S. workers, 25 percent of the national income, and 30 percent of the value added in the Gross National Product.

But most important, manufacturing has a central role to play in the nation's economic future. Its vitality as much as any other sector's will be a major determinant of the nation's overall economic health.

Two basic changes are required, however, if American manufacturing is to play the key economic role it must. First, perceptions must change about manufacturing's present and prospective role in the economy. Indeed, the popular, but false, choice of high-tech versus basic industry is instead one of having a strong manufacturing base (high-tech and basic industries) or a weak and limited manufacturing base. Second, to improve the competitiveness of business we can no longer ignore the fact that—domestically and internationally—government actions affect the vitality of American manufacturing.

MANUFACTURING AND THE ECONOMY

Manufacturing is a major part of the U.S. economy. Specifically, manufacturing added over $772 billion to the GNP in 1980--more than triple its aggregate contribution in 1967. It represents almost 30 percent of the GNP. And a wide array of high-tech and basic industries make these contributions.

Manufacturing also makes a substantial contribution to U.S. national income. In 1981, for example, manufacturing contributed almost one-quarter of total U.S. national income. Its nearest rival was wholesale and retail trade, which contributed 15 percent, almost 40 percent less.

Manufacturing is also a major employment source. Contrary to popular misconception, the levels of manufacturing employment <u>rose</u> by more than 1 million jobs from 1965 to 1981. What has declined is manufacturing employment as a <u>percent</u> of total employment --from 23 to less than 19 percent during this period. Since 1970, employment has grown in such industries as machinery, instruments, lumber and wood, furniture, paper, printing, publishing, petroleum and coal products, rubber and plastics products, stone, clay, and fabricated metals. While absolute levels of manufacturing employment will likely fall in the years immediately ahead, manufacturing will continue to be a major source of good jobs well into the forseeable future.

Most important, the value added created by manufacturing provides the undergirding for much of the economy's balance in such areas as finance, insurance, real estate, transportation, communications, wholesale and retail trade, and other service sectors. Clearly, if the wealth and income created by U.S. manufacturing declines, so too will the related economic activities--unless, of course, substitutes are found. Finding substitutes that can produce over $800 billion annually would, at best, be a difficult task.

The Japanese are now attempting to automate their labor-intensive industries, in large part because of the central economic importance of the value added created by manufacturing. This automation is occurring in such industries as apparel, textiles, and shipbuilding, where the country is losing comparative advantage due to cheaper wage rates in other nations. The Japanese wisely recognize that although the employment in those industries will decline through automation, it is imperative to retain the value added that these industries provide. That value added creates a foundation for service and related industries that can provide substitute employment.

In a like manner, the U.S. economy can't afford to lose its basic industries and the value added they provide. They are too important, and substitute contributors are too difficult to create.

If American manufacturing is going to continue as a strong contributor to the economy, it must go the route of American agriculture: that is, fewer workers, greater productivity, higher volumes of production, and improved quality. Moreover, that process does not mean sacrificing basic American industries such as automobiles and steel. Quite the contrary, it means using technology, such as robots, to make these industries aggressively competitive in domestic and global markets.

Neither does it mean sacrificing total jobs. The retention of the basic production and value added created by more automated industries will create many more new jobs in related industries. Agricultural states, such as Nebraska, have less than 4 percent of their workers engaged in farming, but over a third of all workers are employed in supporting businesses created by farm production. Such can be the case in American manufacturing.

THE COMPETITIVE EDGE

Although the U.S. economy has numerous strengths, there are disturbing signs that its competitive edge is becoming dull. Specifically, productivity growth rates, a key measure of competitiveness, have declined for almost two decades. Firms from Europe and Japan have captured important market shares of non-R&D-intensive products such as steel, shoes, consumer electronics, and automobiles.

The U.S. share of world exports for high-technology products has declined in this past decade from 25 to 20 percent. Since 1965, for example, our world export share of electrical equipment and components has declined from 24 to 17 percent; optical and medical instruments from 20 to 15 percent; plastics and synthetic materials from 20 to 14 percent; drugs and medicines from 23 to 16 percent. Altogether, our world export share of manufactures declined from 25 percent in 1960 to 21 percent today.

The U.S. position in service exports is also declining; in the the past decade, our world trade share in services dropped from 25 to 20 percent.

The point is clear: U.S. competitiveness is slipping and it is not only the older, more mature industries that are facing intense competition, but also the high-tech industries. To meet the global competition, American firms must concentrate on the basics --cost, quality, service, and innovation. While the primary responsibility for this, of course, resides with the private sector, public policies affect how well and at what pace business can proceed. In the quasi-market system under which the U.S. economy operates, there is substantial evidence that firms will respond to opportunities and make changes in response to public policies--macro and micro.

It is also clear that public policies must focus on three areas: capital investment, technological innovation, and the work force's quality of performance. These are the determinants of economic productivity and ultimately of economic competitiveness.

PUBLIC POLICY AND BUSINESS

Abraham Lincoln is alleged to have said that "if your only tool is a hammer, then everything else in the world looks like a nail."

Likewise, many economists and politicians narrowly view fiscal and monetary policies as their only economic tools--that is, the broad manipulation of taxes, expenditures, money supply, and interest rates. This is not to suggest that macroeconomic tools are ineffective, but that their effects are difficult to predict and that there are limits to what fiscal and monetary policies can do. For example, fiscal and monetary policy can not regulate the terms of imports or prevent collusion between firms. It can not stop other nations from creating unfair import barriers or force polluters to stop their polluting practices. And it can not determine which roads and bridges will be built, which harbors will be dredged, and which water and wastewater treatment facilities will be built, or maintain public health and occupational safety.

But there are other tools available to government to take these actions. These tools are known as <u>microeconomic</u> interventions. They include policies and programs for trade and investment, education and training, regulation (including antitrust), natural resources, strategic materials, government subsidies and loans, public works, research and development, and public health, among many others.

When a specific combination of these microeconomic interventions is designed to help urban areas, it is called urban policy. When another combination of micro interventions is aimed at rural places, it is called rural policy.

And when some combination of micro tools is used to help a particular industry develop, compete or adjust, it is called industrial policy--or political economy by the traditionalists. Just as infrastructure is the fashionable new name for public works, industrial policy is the fashionable, although often misunderstood, new name for political economy.

Individual proposals for industrial policy are distinguished by such names as industrial strategy, competitiveness strategy, revitalization strategy, sectoral strategy, reindustrialization, and industrial competitiveness strategy. The confusion and disagreement about the definition of industrial policy arise when a specific proposal--such as Felix Rohatyn's Reconstruction Finance Corporation or the AFL-CIO's reindustrialization program--is viewed (or represented) as the sole approach to industrial policy.

However, to identify any one proposal as the "real" definition of industrial policy is as pointless as equating supply-side economics, Keynesianism, or monetarism as the "real" macroeconomic policy.

Rather, each policy proposal that deals with the way American firms do business has strengths and weaknesses. And each must be evaluated on its own merits. For example, a number of worthwhile proposals have been offered. They include the "American Competitiveness Strategy" of the prestigious Business-Higher Education Forum, a collection of top corporate chief executives and university presidents; and the "industrial strategy" of the influential Committee for Economic Development.

Though there are differences in each of these proposals, they are surprisingly similar. Indeed, these proposals are distinguished not so much by their differences as by their common concerns and assumptions, including:

o While the U.S. economy is not performing nearly as well as most citizens desire, it nevertheless is a strong, vital economy with many strengths. These strengths provide a sound foundation for restoration of long-term, sustainable, noninflationary growth—in other words, the sky is not falling and the nation has the resources, capital, and talent to do what needs to be done.

o There is now a broad agreement that the restoration of long-term, noninflationary, sustainable economic growth depends on the vitality and success of American business, small and large.

o The U.S. economy is no longer closed. In less than two decades, the U.S. economy has changed from a closed economy, with relatively little involvement with trade, to an open economy that is intricately and irreversibly linked with the global economy.

o Enhanced long-term competitiveness—domestically and globally—is central to restoring longer-term vitality to the U.S. economy.

o Improved U.S. productivity is central to improved U.S. competitiveness.

o Restoration of long-term productivity growth will require modernized capital equipment, advances in the creation and commercialization of technology, and improved quality in the work force's performance.

o The activities of business and government are highly interrelated. The decisions of government affect, often profoundly, the decisions of business. Most of the interventions by government that affect business, such as antitrust policy, trade and investment policies, regulatory policies, etc., will continue in the foreseeable future. Thus, the issue is not one of whether government will be involved, but one of how and how much.

o While the activities of business and government are highly interrelated, the extent, degree, and effects of these linkages are only partially known and understood.

The proponents for a national competitiveness strategy recognize that public policy affects the decisions of business through a myriad of techniques—trade barriers, subsidies, government loans, enforced monopolies, protection of nascent industries, market protection, loans and loan guarantees, export assistance, nontariff barriers, grants, tax concessions, insurance, training of workers, procurement of strategic raw materials, and financing of research and development, among dozens of others. They also recognize that governments often try to give their firms an extra (if not unfair) advantage in the marketplace and, at the same time, reduce or offset the advantages given to foreign firms--particularly their unfair advantages.

All nations do this, including the United States. Although not formally identified as such, those policies exist in dozens of U.S. industries, including telecommunications, defense, maritime, trucking, airlines, fisheries, energy, strategic materials, and agriculture.

Thus, the point in the increasingly global competition is not whether these policies exist--they obviously do. Nor is the point that these policies will necessarily ensure economic competitiveness; adequate capital, technology, worker skills, management, service, innovation, quality, price, dedication, pride, and plain hard work are also required.

Rather, the point is that to deny the benefits--and indeed the very existence--of the linkages between public policy and business is to create economic fictions, political barriers, and public misconceptions that hamper the forthright management of government and its economic policies. This denial of reality is a major reason why government interventions in the U.S. economy today are constructed and managed in an ad hoc, inefficient, and costly manner. Furthermore, many of these government interventions have become counterproductive, working against each other and against the nation's longer-term economic interests as well.

Indeed, other nations are becoming competitive in world markets not because they have industrial policies and the United States doesn't, but because they acknowledge the effect of their policies and do a superior job of managing them.

THE NEXT STEPS

The issue of industrial revitalization is moving quickly from the point of whether it's necessary to the more complex and difficult area of how it is to be done.

Government--federal, state, and local--makes a wide and influential array of economic interventions that influence the decisions of business, specific industries, and at times, the performance of the overall economy. Today, there are three pivotal questions involving the management and focus of these micro tools that require attention. First, should some of the micro tools, such as antitrust policy, be modernized? Should other micro interventions be trimmed in some places, perhaps be extended in others, and in virtually all cases be better managed?

Second, how can we make these interventions more internally consistent? For example, should the federal government have a long-term capital investment strategy, as embodied in a capital budget, to help guide its more than $30 billion annual public works investment?

Third, should we focus special attention on how government interventions affect the vitality of a few key industries critical to the nation's long-term interest?

The answer to all three of these questions is a qualified yes. Some existing interventions, such as many regulatory rules and antitrust, require trimming and modernization. Other areas, such as reemployment, retraining, and relocation assistance, also require a more comprehensive, less fragmented effort.

What this means is that we do not need a national planning board which would pick "winners" and "losers" in some bureaucratic competition, but we need to pay closer attention to the effects of the array of economic decisions made by all levels of government. Today a number of key congressional and administration leaders are addressing this need. Specifically, the President has established a National Commission on Industrial Competitiveness, and legislation on worker retraining and anti-trust reform, to take two examples, have been introduced in Congress. While these efforts have some differences, they each are attempts to better manage and better focus what government does, filling gaps where they exist and eliminating interventions that are no longer needed.

An earlier version of this article appeared in the Economic Development Commentary, Winter 1983. Reprinted by permission of Pat Choate.

CHAPTER FOUR:
POLICY RECOMMENDATIONS

Overview

Thomas E. Petri

Whether spurred by the industrial policy debate itself, or the 1980-82 recession, or the problems of particular industries, many groups and individuals have made recommendations in the past several years for improving U.S. industrial competitiveness. Major studies by organizations or commissions alone number at least 25, and many more than that if you include studies more narrowly focused on sub areas like education, research and development, trade, patent law, regulation, or anti-trust.[1]

Broadly based business groups that have issued studies include the Chamber of Commerce, the Business Roundtable, the National Association of Manufacturers, the Committee for Economic Development, and the Computer and Business Equipment Manufacturers Association. Two individual firms, Data Resources, Inc., and the AmeriTrust Corporation, have issued their own reports. Labor is represented by a study from the AFL-CIO's Industrial Union Department. Then there are offerings from seemingly hybrid organizations such as the Labor-Industry Coalition for International Trade and the Business-Higher Education Forum. Think tanks are also represented; examples include reports issued under the auspices of Georgetown University's Center for Strategic and International Studies, and the Heritage Foundation.

Finally, there have been many studies connected with the Federal government. The final report from the President's Commission on Industrial Competitiveness has yet to be issued, but already we have seen studies from the White House Conference on Productivity, the National Productivity Advisory Committee, the National Research Council-National Academy of Sciences, and two efforts from the Department of Commerce. Some would also include in this listing the various recent studies on education, including the most publicized example from the National Commission on Excellence in Education. From the legislative branch we have two nonpartisan studies from the Congressional Budget Office, a staff study from the Joint Economic Committee, reports from the Senate Republican Conference, the House Wednesday Group, the House Republican Research Committee Task Force on High Technology, and the Senate Democratic Policy Committee, and legislation introduced by

John LaFalce (D-NY). Representative LaFalce is Chairman of the House Economic Stablization Subcommittee, which held extensive hearings on industrial policy in 1983.

Among all these efforts, only the LaFalce legislation, the Senate Democratic Policy Committee recommendations, and the AFL-CIO study propose the two core elements of industrial policy: in LaFalce's terminology, a Bank for Industrial Competitiveness and a Council on Industrial Competitiveness to do tripartite planning and coordination addressing specific industries and firms. The Labor-Industry Coalition for International Trade (LICIT), made up of companies and unions in heavily trade-impacted industries like steel, apparel, and electronics, explicitly denies any support for "picking winners and losers," although some of the language in its report undermines substantially those denials.[2] All the other studies avoid endorsing the key components of industrial policy.

The extent to which industrial policy has been discredited today is most apparent in the LICIT report. LICIT is made up of the firms and unions most likely to benefit from any targeted special assistance. Its report endorses "measures for improving access to capital for specific industrial activities or sectors," "special treatment," and "industry-specific measures aimed at addressing the particular circumstances facing individual industries..." Yet it feels compelled to hedge these appeals with dozens of modifiers and qualifications and to state in almost the same breath: "It is highly questionable whether sufficient knowledge exists—much less whether it could be mobilized and the necessary political consensus reached—to read the crystal ball of future industrial competition with the clarity required to pick winners and losers."

Beyond industrial policy as such, however, there is a wide array of suggestions for improving U.S. industrial competitiveness, with a surprising degree of consensus among the various groups. In general, these proposals apply across the board to the basic structure of incentives in the economy. They tend in the direction of improving competition and freeing market forces generally, rather than planning, protecting, and supporting specific sectors. Industrial policy advocates themselves endorse many of them.

At the top of the list is overall monetary and fiscal policy. Everyone agrees we need to keep our economy growing and inflation under control. That is assumed to require stable monetary policy and lowered federal budget deficits, leading to lower federal absorption of credit and lower interest rates. That in turn is supposed to help correct an overvaluation of the U.S. dollar against foreign currencies, making our exports more competitive in world markets and imports more expensive. Although there is universal acceptance of the importance of such macroeconomic policies and the goal of lower deficits in particular, there is little agreement on how to achieve some of these goals.

Beyond basic management of the economy, recommendations fall into the areas of capital formation and taxes, regulation, infrastructure, education and labor, research and development, antitrust policy, and trade. Apart from the Heritage study mentioned earlier, one has to look far to find recommendations in the area of labor law; evidently the expert community is content to let well enough alone there.

Most reports agree that we need to stimulate greater savings and capital formation. Merely attracting huge capital inflows from abroad through high interest rates is regarded as an unsatisfactory substitute in the long run. Of course we have already lowered marginal income tax rates, expanded eligibility for individual retirement accounts, and speeded up depreciation of capital assets in the 1981 tax cuts, all partly in the name of improving capital formation. Further suggestions include simplifying the tax code and broadening the base to achieve further reductions in marginal rates, ending the double taxation of dividends, further expanding IRAs, indexing capital gains for inflation, encouraging employee stock ownership plans (ESOPs), moving toward a consumption tax rather than an income tax, and changing from depreciation to immediate expensing of capital assets.

Expensing of assets is intended not only to stimulate investment, but also to reduce distortions in the allocation of capital to different industries based on their depreciation characteristics. In general, for the marketplace to function most efficiently in allocating resources, government policies should be neutral rather than favoring one industry over another. Currently, however, industries experience widely varying effective tax rates, from 39% to less than zero in one study, due partly to the different depreciation rates of their typical investments. This encourages capital to move into lightly taxed industries in preference to the others, leading to waste and inefficiency.

Many other government activities affect the allocation of capital—directly and indirectly. These should be consolidated, made as neutral as possible, and probably reduced. One little known source of federal capital allocation is the Federal Financing Bank, an agency in the Treasury Department that finances lending by Federal agencies. Incredibly, since 1975 this agency has financed over $125 BILLION in net agency loans, $100 BILLION of which is called "off-budget spending" and translates directly into increased Federal borrowing in the credit markets. This spending is not appropriated by Congress, and Congress is not required to raise revenue or cut other programs to finance it.

Recommendations on regulation fall into two areas: deregulating particular industries to improve competition, and reviewing social and environmental regulation to make it more cost-effective and efficient. In recent years, we have made substantial progress in deregulating trucking, the airlines, railroads, bus companies, oil, financial institutions, and communications services, with generally impressive gains in competition and efficiency. More could be accomplished in several of these industries, as well as natural gas, agriculture, insurance on the state level, and removing barriers to coal slurry pipelines. In many cases, misguided regulation has directly harmed our trade balance. A good example is the government's tobacco monopoly, which has priced our tobacco out of world markets and caused a deterioration of several billion dollars per year in our trade balance over the past decade.

A related item which none of the studies mentions is health care costs, which have exploded to over 10% of total GNP and add to costs in every other industry through employee health insurance. Chrysler Corporation reports that health care expenses now add $600 to the cost of every car it sells. Health care is also placing enormous pressure on the federal budget. In this case, the problem has resulted not from regulation per se, but from predominant third party payment mechanisms which remove incentives to control costs. The solution is to reform these arrangements to introduce more competition and market incentives. A great ferment of ideas is already proceeding in the private sector, including health maintenance organizations, preferred provider arrangements, innovative patient cost sharing, wellness programs, and others. Since the government now sets the framework for nearly half of all health expenditures in the country, it can contribute immensely by making its own programs more economically sensible.

Almost all the studies recommend that social and environmental regulations should be reviewed for cost effectiveness. Everyone shares the goals of clean air and water, workplace safety and health, product safety, non-discrimination in employment, pension plan protection, and so on. The question is how best to achieve them. Clean air laws that mandate a particular percentage reduction of sulphur regardless of the original sulphur content of the coal are one example of inefficient regulation. In this case, the law was written not to clean the air most effectively, but to protect the producers of high sulphur coal. The law should mandate an absolute emission standard and let the market determine how best to meet it, whether by burning cleaner coal, experimenting with new technologies, or trading emissions among boilers. Better yet, we could consider taxing pollution if we could work out the implementation.

Inadequate roads, ports, sewer systems, and other infrastructure can also add to industrial costs, so a couple of the studies recommend greater governmental expenditures in this area. Again, however, it is more important to spend wisely than to spend heavily, especially with our deficit problem in mind. Unfortunately, much of our federal public works spending supports projects that are economic pygmies but political giants. We should fundamentally reform our decision making on public works by requiring local and user cost sharing on all projects, so that we fund only those which can command some financial support on their economic merits.

One of the most critical inputs to all industries is an educated and productive labor force. Almost everyone agrees we need to make dramatic improvements in our education systems through such ideas as merit pay for teachers, tougher course loads and standards for students, principal training, curriculum reform, and the like. One idea not mentioned as often is competition among schools--giving parents and students a choice among schools, either within a public system or even between public and private schools. Several public systems have had good results with this approach, since it shows which schools are best, provides justification for changing or closing the worst, and provides greater opportunity particularly for lower-income students.

Once workers are in the labor force, they should be able to retrain for new skills when necessary. Especially when their old jobs disappear, public programs should encourage them to retrain for new jobs rather than to remain on income maintenance programs indefinitely. The new Job Training Partnership Act should be an improvement in this regard. We could also use a computerized national job bank so that displaced workers could more easily move to where the jobs are rather than relying on new jobs to come to where the workers are.

Most studies place a high priority on support for research and development efforts. Most maintain that the federal government should concentrate its efforts on basic research and increase funding in that area. There are several ideas for tax incentives to encourage private research and cooperation between corporations and universities. There are also several patent law suggestions, such as expanding patent protection for process improvements and for intellectual property, including software and microchip designs. An expanded effort to survey foreign technological developments and make information on them available to U.S. firms could also be very useful. We should examine thoroughly all suggestions concerning research and development since this is one of the fundamental engines of economic progress and international competitiveness.

One way to facilitate large R&D efforts is to allow several firms to cooperate on them without running afoul of our antitrust laws. That seems reasonable if there is no collusion or monopolization in the use of the results, and it is supported by most of the studies. Several other suggestions have been offered to prevent unnecessary antitrust actions where there is easy entry into the industry or substantial international competition.

Finally, there is a wide variety of suggestions in the area of trade, for it is perceived trade problems and imbalances that give rise to the whole industrial policy debate in the first place. The most widely supported recommendation is for the U.S. to take a tougher stance in international trade negotiations for removing barriers to free trade generally. There are several suggestions for responding to alleged unfair or predatory foreign practices, but these are more controversial.

It should not be controversial to take stronger measures against international counterfeiters, as suggested by the Senate Republican Conference study. Likewise, there is broad support for doing a better job of gathering information on developments in other countries and their possible effects on U.S. trade. Again, it doesn't seem sensible to prohibit export of products that meet the standards of other countries but not our own. Why abandon markets in other countries to foreign firms willing to supply what those markets want?

Two other suggestions are already being implemented by our government. We are encouraging the formation of export trading companies to facilitate exporting by smaller companies, and we are urging Japan to internationalize the yen, which should lead eventually to a more realistic exchange rate against the dollar.

Clearly we have a large menu of proposals for improving U.S. industrial competitiveness. This discussion has only touched on the selections and added a few that seem to be missing from other lists. The following articles from John Young, Chairman of the President's Commission on Industrial Competitiveness, and from the Committee for Economic Development, provide thoughtful and specific suggestions for improving our economy. These and other studies remind us that proposals to improve our economy are not limited to the simplistic reforms which have characterized industrial policy. If we take this message to heart, we need not fear foreign competition.

NOTES

1. See Bibliography, Part IV., Policy Recommendations, p. 169.

2. Labor Industry Coalition for International Trade, "International Trade, Industrial Policies, and the Future of American Industry," (1983), pp. 62-64, especially the three paragraphs beginning on the fourth to last line of p.63.

How to Improve the Competitiveness of American Industry

John A. Young

Certainly the ability of American business to compete—both at home and abroad—has broad consequences for all Americans. We face major structural changes in the world economy, and the wisdom with which we respond to these new challenges will affect the well-being of future generations.

For that reason, we cannot afford to consider competitiveness a partisan issue. Our continued success in world markets will require the best efforts of all of us—and then some. We need to realize that we all—Republicans and Democrats, management and labor, smokestack and high-technology—have more interests in common than we might have presumed. It's time to recognize and build on those shared interests.

The attention recently given to the competitiveness question is healthy and can lead to some constructive development. I'm not so sure that the issue would have received any attention as little as five years ago. It is a positive first step for us to have recognized the significance of the change we're experiencing. The sheer volume of world trade has grown dramatically in the last decade, and our own economy has a growing international character.

Both our private and public sectors have been slow to recognize and respond to this change. Perhaps this lack of response is a measure of how much we have managed to insulate ourselves from the realities of world competition.

A PERSPECTIVE ON COMPETITIVENESS ISSUES

My involvement in the competitiveness issue started with my role as head of Hewlett-Packard Company, an electronics company that participates quite heavily in foreign markets. About half our sales are abroad, and we are one of the nation's twenty leading exporters.

We also participate in an industry that faces increasingly focused and concerted foreign competition. The industry has seen a strong Japanese incursion into its semiconductor segment—a sector which provides the basic building blocks for all electronic products. The nation has also experienced an increasing American trade deficit in consumer electronic products. These trends, combined with HP's strong international presence, have caused me to give a great deal of thought to what factors contribute to the competitiveness--or uncompetitiveness of an industry.

My philosophical home base is the view that the final test of whether a product or industry is competitive rests in the world marketplace. That means that the responsibility for being competitive rests primarily with the private sector, where decisions are made about what will be produced, the markets served, and the cost and quality of the products offered.

THE GOVERNMENT POLICY FRAMEWORK

What government does, however, affects what resources are available to the private sector and the decisions it makes. Government policy--whether fiscal, social or international--represents the framework within which the private sector operates. In the past, we have often neglected to ask how those policies affect our competitive position, and it is now appropriate to examine those relationships in detail.

A review of the governmental framework, however, should not be predicated on the assumption that government action alone can counteract or determine trends in the world market. Government's proper role is to encourage the activities that will contribute to the competitiveness of the private sector rather than to implicitly encourage or discourage selected industrial sectors. No amount of government support can ensure commercial success. Take the Concorde jet as an example. The British and French governments spent vast amounts of money in its development, but it was a commercial failure. The market rejected it.

This analysis is not meant to suggest that the world market is not often distorted by our own activities and those of our trading partners. We often find ourselves playing on a field that is far from level, and we need to find ways to bring things more into balance. But the cost, quality, and appropriateness of the goods and services we offer are the primary determinants of our success in world markets. And these factors are most influenced by the private sector.

FOUR COMPETITIVENESS ISSUE AREAS IDENTIFIED

A great number of studies have already been done on the question of what makes American industry competitive, and we have defined four basic areas. These are 1) human resources, 2) capital resources, 3) innovation and the production process, and 4) the laws and practices of international trade and marketing. The President's Commission on Industrial Competitiveness, which I have been privileged to chair, and which is charged with reviewing means of increasing the long-term competitiveness of U.S. industries both at home and abroad, is also organized in committees along these lines, and those committees are currently developing work plans for their efforts. With this work in the formative stages, I can't fully anticipate what issues the committee will address. However, there are some key areas which I'm sure will be reviewed.

As I discuss each of these four areas, I'll start from the vantage point of what the private sector needs to do to remain competitive. I will then discuss public policy issues which either contribute or detract from industry's competitive ability.

HUMAN RESOURCES

In the area of human resources, the private sector—both management and labor—should do three things. First, it needs to attract and motivate a qualified workforce. Then it needs to maintain and develop the skills of the workforce it has employed. Lastly, industry must create an atmosphere where management and employees are working for the same goals and where the risks and rewards of their business are shared equitably.

These fundamental human resource requirements point to changes needed in both the public and private sectors. Our educational system needs a great deal of attention. We should be teaching our people how to learn. We can't predict, with any certitude, exactly what skills will be needed in the workforce of the future.

A better focus for our educational system would be a sound grounding in basic skills, with an emphasis on lifelong learning to adapt to new technologies and new markets. We'll simply have to discard the notion that education is something that can be pursued for a short, prescribed period of life and then never revisited.

I hesitate to give you too much detail on the plight of our educational system. The Business-Higher Education Forum and the National Commission on Excellence in Education have well portrayed the severity of the crisis—declining test scores, poorly prepared and poorly paid teachers, and as one report put it, a threat of mediocrity.

From my own vantage point as a particpant in an industry where innovation and knowledgeable people are the prime resource, I find it troubling that the Japanese produce two-and-a half times as many engineers per capita as we do. The engineering faculty shortage in this nation's universities is acute. If this problem is not addressed, our ability to maintain America's technological leadership is seriously jeopardized.

I also think that high school graduation requirements of just one year of math and science are a mistake. The age of 15 or 16 is just too young to effectively close off career options, and yet many of our young people have, in essence, been allowed to attenuate their own participation in a wide range of career options.

The educational problem is amply identified; the solutions remain to be enacted. And yet here is an area with the widest possible implications, affecting the entire range of U.S. industry.

EMPLOYEE/MANAGEMENT RELATIONS

Still on the subject of human resources, the private sector needs to take a look at ways to create a congruence of interests within its organizations. The best results are obtained when everyone--management and labor--has a unifying goal. One thing that has certainly struck me about our Japanese competitors is the strength of their unified purpose.

I think there are ways management can foster such sharing of goals. Among them are profit-sharing, employee stock purchase programs, and open lines of communication. At HP, we have a practice we call managing-by-wandering-around. We don't just sit in our offices. We get up and go where the action is, and we learn a lot that way. We also have no doors on our offices, and this encourages a lot of drop-in visits. Sometimes more than we'd like, but we know that the accessibility and informality we aim to foster have some real business benefits.

Employee groups also have a responsibility for responding to our competitive challengers. Especially important is a mind-set that is open to change and able to respond to new market forces and technologies. Workers have to confront the reality that, in the end, their jobs depend on the ability of their organization to compete in world markets. Nothing is going to change that, no matter how strongly we may wish otherwise.

INNOVATION AND THE PRODUCTION PROCESS

In the area of innovation and the production process, America's lead is under serious pressure. To remain competitive, industry must be able to innovate and to manage risk and change. It must also be able to offer products and services that are competitive in price and quality. This very fundamental challenge --the price and quality of our products--means that industry must invest in ways to make its employees more productive.

PRODUCTIVITY

Improving employee productivity is the only way we are going to retain jobs here in America. Since some of our trading partners have lower wage scales--for employees of all ranks--our only logical alternative is to make the U.S. workforce worth more. And that means investing in productivity-improving equipment and training our workforce to use it effectively.

When the President's Commission on Industrial Competitiveness first defined the subject areas to be pursued, we had two separate catagories. The first was labeled research and development and the second was the production process. We decided to combine those two areas, and the reasoning behind the combination is illustrative of one central theme which cannot be ignored.

As a nation, we have not done enough research and development on the production process. Our Japanese competitors have certainly honed their expertise in this area, and we can see the results in the cost and quality of their products. Jim Baker, an executive vice president of General Electric Company, has described the Japanese approach so well that I'd like to quote him: "They have discovered that if you can't make a better product, you learn to make a product better." And that means more reliable or less expensive than your competitor—or ideally, both.

FEDERAL R&D

The area of innovation and the production process is one where the private sector bears the bulk of the responsibility, but public policies can be helpful in two ways. First, there should be increased federal support for basic research performed at the university level and a better focus for the federally funded R&D that we undertake. Collaborative research vehicles—pooling the resources of government, industry, and academia—should be established to pursue basic research in areas of potential commercial applications. Our universities are strapped for funds and equipment, and such collaborative research would enable them to retain the innovative leadership of America.

We should also streamline the management of our federal labs and improve the focus of their efforts. The President's Private Sector Survey on Cost Control undertook a study of more than 700 federal research laboratories. Headed by Dave Packard, the group concluded that the labs often have research goals that are poorly defined or frequently changing directions.

The group also described a managerial maze few scientists are able to navigate—more than 2,700 distinct federal R&D programs receiving line-by-line budget scrutiny from 54 different Congressional committees and subcommittees. Since federal funds comprise about half of total R&D spending in this country, better focus and management of that effort would be extremely beneficial.

PRIVATE SECTOR R&D

Governmental policies also affect R&D activities in the private sector, and those policies should encourage these activities. I've seen analyses that compare the trade balance of industries that are research-intensive to those that are not. The contrast is quite apparent. Industries that spend a large percentage of their revenues on R&D have a positive trade balance. Industries that spend comparatively little, on the other hand, show a trade deficit.

We should review our tax policies for their effects on R&D spending, develop ways to protect intellectual property, and exempt certain kinds of joint research ventures from anti-trust actions. Certainly, the R&D tax credit passed in 1981 has proved a significant incentive to private sector efforts. The credit should be made permanent.

Moving to the area of capital resources, there is a need for American industry to develop a long-term investment prospective, where the goal of business activity is to produce real wealth rather than manipulate paper assets. Industry should also be encouraged to invest in plants and equipment that will increase our ability to compete by increasing the productivity of our work force.

The investment and long-term perspective we desire are, of course, directly affected by what is happening to U.S. interest rates. Some studies put U.S. capital costs at twice those faced by our international competitors. These high interest rates also contribute to the strength of the U.S. dollar, and the strong dollar has really hurt the competitiveness of U.S. products sold abroad.

The U.S.-Japan Advisory Commission, headed by Dave Packard, recently issued an interim report advocating a 40-yen adjustment in the exchange rate between the dollar and the yen. Such a move, in the Commission's view, would aid considerably in reducing the large, bilateral trade deficit we have with Japan and increase our ability to compete with the Japanese in foreign markets.

Packard cites high U.S. interest rates as one of the prime factors contributing to the yen-dollar exchange rate problem. I'd like to quote Mr. Packard's comment on this issue, because he has a way of getting to the heart of things: "Everybody in the Congress and government knows that interest rates are too high, but for political reasons nobody wants to do anything about it."

What we're talking about here, of course, is a macro-economic issue adversely affecting a broad segment of American industry. While we address the problem, I suggest we also look for ways to increase the efficiency and flexibility of the capital markets. New financing mechanisms such as tax-deductible preferred stock issues are possibilities worth exploring. The venture capital market has been doing well because of the lowered capital gains tax rate, but there is a need for more capital for mid-sized companies.

INTERNATIONAL TRADE

Let me move on to the murkiest of areas we face in the competitiveness arena, and that is the subject of international trade. I mentioned earlier that American business should ideally compete on a level playing field where the market reflects the success with which an industry can offer innovative products and services of reasonable cost and quality. Unfortunately, we exist in a world where debt-strapped developing countries, as well as our industrial trading partners, have adopted conscious strategies to maximize exports and minimize imports. As a result, we are operating in a market that is often distorted.

I don't have a simple answer to how to deal with a world trade arena that is becoming increasingly important and complex. I believe we'll have to strengthen and broaden the General Agreement on Tariffs and Trade. It's also time to review current U.S. trade laws to determine if they are adequate to respond to the export promotion practices of our trading partners. Beyond being adequate, they should be easily enforced—and in a timely manner.

Promoting open markets abroad is only half of the international trade agenda. We should also encourage exports of American products through better export financing, reasonable export control policies, and tax policies. Here the private sector has a role to play. Too often, American industry has hesitated to look beyond its own borders for potential markets. We are prone to a kind of provincialism that we can no longer afford.

It is most apparent that these attitudes and many of our past beliefs and practices are no longer appropriate. On that point, I believe we have consensus. This nation is at a crossroads. We recognize that we are no longer the automatic world leader in all market segments. We also recognize that we must take stock of our strengths and weaknesses—do a kind of national audit on our competitive position and its underpinnings.

I took on the role of chairing the President's Commission on Industrial Competitiveness because I believe that we can strengthen the performance of American industry both at home and abroad. I don't think there's a single, simple solution for the challenges we face. But I think we can reach a constructive consensus on what needs to be accomplished and whether that task is best undertaken in the private or public sector.

The enormity of the challenge we face—put into the context of an election year—makes it very tempting to look for the simple, grand strategy or slogan to solve all our ills. Let us resist that temptation. We can't wait for the definitive solution, the grand plan. We have enough trouble agreeing on the definitions of what we're doing, much less the content of those strategies.

I believe that effective policy decisions are incremental in nature. That seems to be the pace at which U.S. history is most comfortably made. Let's identify some areas already identified. Let's be sure that the remedies we select really fit the problems we've identified and the political and economic context in which we operate.

From a statement printed in the Congressional Record, November 17, 1983, p.H 10366-68. Reprinted by permission of John A. Young.

Strategy for U.S. Industrial Competitiveness

Committee for Economic Development

The era of unquestioned U.S. dominance in the world economy is clearly over, and has been for some time. The combined forces of lagging U.S. productivity performance and the rising competitiveness of other countries leave us with no choice but to adopt policies to strengthen our competitive position if we wish to increase the real economic well-being of the American people and maintain our position as a leading economic power in the world.

Neither further government involvement in the economy nor new policies or institutions designed to steer the economy in some predetermined direction will increase U.S. competitiveness. Rather, the most effective, and perhaps the only successful, path to increased U.S. international competitiveness is through (a) placing significantly more reliance on free market forces, and (b) reforming necessary government interventions to provide an economic environment which stimulates innovation in the private sector and helps resources adapt to changing competition. Increased interference with the market economy will weaken it further, harming business, workers, and consumers alike.

Structural economic change, through technological advances, shifts in consumer preferences and the growing importance of a global economy, is a continuous process. Over time the relative importance of some industrial sectors in the economy declines, but this does not mean that the U.S. industrial base will be eroded or that our manufacturing capability will inevitably decline.

The contribution of manufacturing to the output of the economy has remained relatively stable over the past two decades, even as service producing industries have become slightly more important. Continuous economic change, however, has redistributed the labor force among major industrial sectors. Even though in absolute terms manufacturing employment grew during the past two decades, its relative share of nonagricultural employment declined chiefly because of the surge in service employment. This shift in employment distribution was most pronounced during the 1960s, not the 1970s.

Since 1980 we have experienced the most severe setback in economic activity in the post-World War II period. The service-producing sectors have continued to grow in relative importance as a source of both output and employment. On the other hand, goods-producing industries—and especially manufacturing industries which are very sensitive to changes in economic activity—lost both employment and share of the labor force after 1980. A strong recovery from the recent recession has rapidly expanded employment in the goods-producing industries, and government projections predict that manufacturing employment will continue to expand through 1990. It is not yet clear, however, whether this recession has produced any _major_ permanent change in the structure of the economy. What _is_ certain is that significant changes in the employment distribution of industries _within_ manufacturing and nonmanufacturing sectors will continue throughout the remainder of this decade, and may prove to be more rapid than in the past.

Judged by total output comparisons, the U.S. economy is not "deindustrializing" but important structural changes have occurred _within_ sectors of the economy and some industries and firms have lost competitiveness. Neither a strong economic recovery nor more favorable exchange rates achieved through improved general economic policies will fully restore the former competitive position of many of these firms. At the same time, some industries in both the manufacturing and nonmanufacturing sectors have improved their competitive position and are now more important sources of output and employment growth.

Of course, it makes no economic sense for U.S. companies to try to be leading competitors in _every_ industry. But since productivity growth rates in some U.S. industries have been consistently lower than comparable rates of growth in other nations for two decades, the _level_ of productivity in one U.S. manufacturing industry after another has been matched and in some cases surpassed by our major competitors. This has been a significant source of the serious and growing loss of competitiveness in some sectors of the U.S. economy.[2] It is difficult to determine the competitive position of industries in the nonmanufacturing sector, but persistent low productivity growth in most of these industries should be a warning that many nonmanufacturing industries are also likely to face increasing competition from foreign rivals.

Our recent history of high rates of inflation, poor productivity, prolonged exchange rate misalignment and high levels of unemployment are all related to loss of competitiveness and are, of course, causes for very serious concern. During the strong domestic recovery of 1983-1984, we have made significant progress in reversing some of these trends, but many of the structural problems underlying our deteriorating competitiveness have not yet been solved. For many sectors of the U.S. economy, the need to revitalize competitiveness has reached the stage of urgency.

The sharply increased price of energy since 1973, the shifting consumer appetite for smaller and imported cars, rising real interest rates, the changing comparative advantage of Japanese, German, and U.S. firms--these and many other developments were of of a scope and speed that were simply not foreseen in our economy. While many of these changes were largely beyond the control of both private-sector and government policies, some important sources of the current U.S. competitiveness problems can be traced to past and present public policies. U.S. economic policy has long favored consumption over saving and investment, with the result that the investment in future economic growth has been inhibited. Compared to our major industrial competitors the United States has consistently had lower rates of private saving and investment, and in real terms there was little net increase in investment in U.S. manufacturing plant and equipment during 1973-1979. This has contributed importantly to the loss of competitiveness in some U.S. industries.

There has also been a strong current consumption bias in public expenditures. During the 1960s, government transfer payments and grants-in-aid increased at about eight percent a year in real terms. This average annual rate of growth in social transfers continued into the 1970s despite a significant decline in productivity growth and a slowing of real economic growth to a little over three percent a year. In addition, the growth of the public sector has had the effect of "crowding out" some private sector investment, and government interferences with the price system in some major areas of the economy have resulted in a misallocation of resources without any net social benefit.

To bolster the performance of all sectors of the economy, the challenge now is to develop concrete, constructive public policies to enable the economy to adapt better to emerging trends with less delay, fewer inefficiencies, and less contradictory actions. Future policies should focus on how to provide individuals with the skills to be flexible in labor markets of the future and how to motivate investors and managers to shift labor and capital resources smoothly toward expanding markets and away from less competitive ones. In short, this nation needs a strategy toward all industries that avoids protecting the status quo and, instead, facilitates adjustment so that the nation can capture the advantages of structural change. With appropriate public and private policy changes, the United States and its trading partners will be in a better position to realize the long-run benefits of expanding international trade in an increasingly interdependent world.

CED'S VIEW OF A COMPETITIVE STRATEGY

Governments in all developed economies try to raise industrial output, employment, and productivity. In some countries, the goals of these policies are relatively explicit. Some have a stated coordinated strategy of long-term government planning, designating which industries and regions will be assisted. For most countries, however, industrial policies are not comprehensive; they consist of a combination of separate economic development policies, investment incentives, and protection of specific industries from foreign competition.

Recently, there have been calls from a variety of groups with differing political persuasions for the United States to adopt an "industrial policy." Most of these proposals recommend increased government intervention in markets to affect the pace of economic change and provide preferential government assistance to specific industries and groups of workers.[3]

Some industrial policy proposals advocate the establishment of new institutions that would have authority to divert government expenditures and private pension fund assets, and provide preferential loans and tax incentives to assist specific industries and firms. The overall direction of the strategy would be determined to an important extent by a tripartite Industrial Development Board, consisting of representatives of labor, business, and government. Some proponents claim that Industrial Development Board decisions would be only advisory, but at the same time, the board would be responsible for determining the key sectors and regions of the economy that deserve assistance. Management of the targeted assistance program would be in the hands of a new institution, similar in concept to the Japan Development Board or a reconstituted Reconstruction Finance Corporation. This new independent financial institution would include tripartite representation and would carry out the policies emanating from the Industrial Development Board. Some supporters of this form of market intervention envisage an extensive network of industry and regional boards similar to the approach adopted by the United Kingdom during the 1970s. These boards would have significant power in the allocation of government assistance to specific industries and companies. <u>This Committee strongly opposes such a strategy for improving U.S. competitiveness.</u>

Whenever interested parties participate directly and collectively in public policy decisions affecting economic change, there is a strong tendency toward agreement on policies that favor the status quo and impede economic change. And it is likely that those with new ideas will be underrepresented in such collective decision making. The goal of improving U.S. competitiveness thus becomes more difficult to achieve because resources tend to be retained in those economic activities and in firms and industries in which productivity growth is lowest. There is no evidence that a tripartite group of individuals representing diverse interests will be more successful than the market system in identifying the industries and companies which are crucial to the future success of the economy. In fact, U.S. experience has shown that targeted governmental assistance has typically been based on political expediency rather than economic potential.

In sharp contrast with increased government targeting to sectors and regions, <u>CED emphasizes more reliance on the market</u> system for identifying promising industries and permitting economic activity to decline where firms have lost their basic comparative advantage. The market system's signals indicate the direction of the forthcoming change while relative price changes provide a strong incentive for management and labor to adjust to industrial, occupational, and geographic changes. If the government resists pressure to intervene in these markets, the market system will in most cases provide gradual structural change.[4]

Over the years, CED has stressed consistently the importance of relying on relative market prices as much as possible for reallocating resources. If the market system is to guide resource allocation, public policies affecting industry should be as neutral as possible and avoid favoring specific sectors of the economy.

A COMPETITIVE MARKET ECONOMY: COMPONENTS OF CED's APPROACH

For society to benefit most from continuous structural change in product and labor markets, government must adopt a policy strategy which enables capital and labor resources to move to their most efficient use. CED believes that a competitive market economy is the essential foundation of such a strategy because experience in most industrial nations has shown that "it is normally the best mechanism to marshal responses to social, economic and technological changes, flexibly, constructively and without excessive cost."[5]

Under CED's market-based strategy the prime responsibility for improving competitiveness rests with the private sector—both managers and their employees. The market system rewards firms that innovate, anticipate changes in demand, and restructure their resources to meet or overtake foreign competition; it penalizes those that fail to adopt new productive techniques, improve quality, reduce unit costs of production, pursue new markets, or take account of the long-term implications of managerial decisions. The major responsibility for actions to increase the speed with which capital and labor resources are reallocated to their most efficient use falls on management and labor. In a market-based strategy, compensation inflexibility, barriers to labor mobility, and hiding behind a wall of protectionism when competitiveness is lost are all detrimental to society, and eventually to those adversely affected by economic change.[6]

Although competitive markets are crucial to the efficient reallocation of resources, they do not always work perfectly. Government policies can improve market performance by reducing restrictions, such as unnecessary market regulations, and by minimizing distortions when government is likely to produce some undesirable social result.

In addition, government intervention to improve the operation of markets can be legitimate when markets fail. However, such intervention should be undertaken only if the result of the government action (including the cost) is likely to be superior to the outcome of an imperfectly functioning market.[7]

Public policies should not attempt to halt or modify the pace of structural change. On the contrary, policies should be as neutral as possible in their effect on the allocation of resources. Similarly, when interventions are necessary to assist those hurt by change, the policy instruments should not attempt to preserve the status quo. Public and private policies should be designed to encourage labor and capital resources to adapt so that the benefits of change can be widely distributed throughout society.[8]

RECOMMENDATIONS

1. **Economic and Strategic Environment for Providing U.S. Competitiveness**

The basis for any set of strategies to improve U.S. competitiveness must be government policies aimed at achieving sustained, noninflationary economic growth. We urge actions that will encourage such growth. This requires policies that will gradually but substantially reduce the level of projected future FEDERAL BUDGET DEFICITS.

Reducing deficits will require a further reduction in the growth of public expenditures. The size of the projected deficit will also make it necessary to raise additional revenue but it is important to avoid tax increases that discourage productive investment. Unless steps are taken to bring about a sharp reduction in budget deficits over the next few years, inflation risks will rise, capital investment will be discouraged, and the prospects of future economic growth will be impaired. Anticipation of these possibilities may already be adversely affecting investment decisions.

In order to reduce the growth of FEDERAL EXPENDITURES, all programs, including national defense, should be reexamined for both soundness and cost effectiveness. Although some direct program cuts may be possible, much of the future reduction in expenditures will have to come from limiting the growth of existing programs. We recommend that future benefit increases in entitlement programs (including Social Security) be less rapid than the rate of inflation while protecting the income security of the poor. We also recommend that the increase in defense buildup be less rapid than now proposed. As the economy moves to a relatively high level of output, the long-term goal of FISCAL POLICY should be to eliminate the federal deficit.

In general, the tax code should be reformed in ways that remove the current biases which favor consumption and discourage saving and investment. We urge consideration of some form of tax simplification that could broaden the tax base, lower rates, and provide more neutrality between incentives for individuals to consume and save. To make business taxes more neutral in the way income from different types of capital assets is taxed, we recommend that some form of expensing (i.e., immediate deductibility of of business capital investment) be considered for all plant and equipment, including research and development (R&D) capital.[9]

EXCHANGE RATE POLICY is critically important to competitiveness because, as recent experience shows, significant changes in the rate of exchange can alter the prices of U.S.-produced goods and services sold abroad and the prices of imported goods sold in the U.S. market. We urge development of an appropriate U.S. exchange rate policy that gives adequate consideration to both macroeconomic measures and other actions which may produce a more favorable exchange rate. We encourage continued study of the practicality of government purchases and sales of foreign exchange timed to help dampen large swings in the dollar's value. Limited government operations in foreign exchange markets should be considered as these studies proceed.

NATIONAL SECURITY must be a basic component of any set of industrial strategies. Much of the nation's security rests on a strong industrial base and on the ability of U.S. industry to supply basic materials in a military emergency. The government should identify a list of critical components for a military emergency and should estimate the national security threshold of domestic production of these components.

In addition, supplies and stockpiles of critical materials and machine tools must be built up. The President, the Department of Commerce, and the Department of Defense should exercise their existing authority to stockpile strategic materials in order to meet realistic national security goals.

Export of certain technologies can pose real security threats. We support government approval of exports if they result in a transfer of technological know-how which is truly critical to national security and can be controlled through government regulation. If U.S. exports to countries in the free world involve routine commodities and technical data without any effective transfer of technology, advance government approval should not be required.

2. Facilitating Industrial, Regional, and Labor Market Adjustments

Any approach to improving U.S. competitiveness must address the issue of various types of government assistance to companies, industries, and regions whose competitiveness is declining and to dislocated workers.

In general, we believe that GOVERNMENT TARGETING of domestic policies is NOT an effective mechanism for stimulating innovation and that well-intentioned subsidies to improve investment in specific industries should be reversed. If future subsidies are deemed justified, they should be directed to industries rather than specific companies and should be designed to give labor and capital the time to move over to other economic activities. Such assistance should be phased out according to a designated time schedule.

We do not believe that federal programs should be targeted to help specific areas of the country. Rather, we favor general programs designed to aid any local area in serious economic difficulty, with decisions on how such assistance should be utilized made at the local level.

During structural change, government can play a role in the retraining and relocation of permanently displaced workers. We offer specific recommendations for IMPROVING THE EFFECTIVENESS AND FLEXIBILITY OF THE NATION'S UNEMPLOYMENT INSURANCE SYSTEM to encourage workers to seek new employment and to make retraining more accessible. In the event of PLANT CLOSINGS, industries should have the flexibility to adopt voluntarily the appropriate mix of responses including prenotification, severance pay, benefit extension, and cooperation with public-sector training and relocation programs.

We believe that the greatest threat to employment security comes from failure to innovate. Growth, innovation, and increased competitiveness offer far more hope for increased employment than does protection of failing or noncompetitive industries.

3. The Role of Regulatory and Antitrust Policies in a Competitive Society

The government's regulation of economic activities has a direct bearing on U.S. world competitiveness. In general, much GOVERNMENT REGULATION, especially social regulation, is in need of significant reform. These reforms should concentrate on better balancing of regulation's costs and benefits, a more realistic appraisal of the effects of regulation, and the use of market incentives whenever possible.

Although fundamental changes in antitrust laws are not called for, a number of statutory and enforcement reforms are needed. In recognition of the growing interdependence of the INTERNATIONAL ECONOMY, all relevant government authorities should include in their analyses of market competition those firms, including foreign competitors, that are active competitors in the domestic market being analyzed. This is especially important in reviewing joint research proposals and proposed mergers. Mergers are frequently the most effective way to achieve industrial restructuring in a market economy. Unless such mergers occur there is a serious risk that pressure for protection will increase.

Congress should maintain the normal prohibition against HORI-

ZONTAL PRICE-FIXING and grant exemptions only if the proposed exemption would lead to more competition and would not lead to future collusion.

We support the Justice Department's proposal to test the appropriate limits on VERTICAL PRICE ARRANGEMENTS. If a proper rule of reason cannot be put in place without statutory change, the Administration should submit legislation on this issue.

To streamline ANTITRUST ENFORCEMENT, Congress should consider broadening the precedent created by the Export Trading Act of 1982, which requires that private plaintiffs pay the cost of unsuccessful antitrust actions. In addition, extension of the clearance process created in the Export Trading Act to certain joint ventures should be considered.

A unique aspect of U.S. antitrust litigation is the ability of the injured private parties to collect automatically three times demonstrated damages. Congress should limit such triple damages to cases in which the conduct is per se illegal and carried out in secret. At the very least, judges should have discretion in multiple-damages awards.

4. Adjusting to Changing International Competitiveness

We now turn to the issue of government responsibility toward industries that are threatened by imports and the question of how to reconcile restrictive national trade actions with efficient and equitable functioning of an interdependent world economy. Many countries, including the United States, use import restrictions to protect certain domestic industries. Escape clauses allow the imposition of import restrictions that would otherwise not be permitted. For the United States, we recommend that granting the escape-clause protection should be treated as an unusual exception to the general policy of treating firms as risk-taking enterprises and allowing firms to succeed or fail on the basis of traditional market principles.

On a broader scale, it is vital that an effective international safeguard code be negotiated and implemented. Subjecting restrictive trade actions to international review and discipline would make it easier for all countries to resist direct protectionist measures.

There should be a long-term effort for the General Agreement for Trade and Tariffs (GATT) to restrain the growing use of foreign investment incentives and performance requirements.

A number of the more economically advanced developing countries are ready to graduate to full responsibility in the international trading community. In order to encourage this process, GATT should establish a Committee on Graduation to develop criteria to encourage the more developed Third World countries to accept the rules applying to mature international trading partners.

5. Unfair International Competition

While remedies already exist in international guidelines to deal with the problems of dumping and foreign government subsidization of exports, they should be enforced more vigorously and expeditiously than in the past. When foreign governments provide their companies with DOMESTIC SUBSIDIES that do not differentiate between sales in their domestic market and sales abroad, U.S. competitiveness is damaged by this advantage. We suggest that, although domestic subsidies are acceptable under GATT, they should be identified and effective remedies for subsidization affecting competition in third-country markets should be developed. New international guidelines are also needed to deal with the problems of nations targeting particular domestic industries for special assistance and support.

In dealing with STATE ENTERPRISES, if the new GATT codes on subsidies and dumping prove inadequate for dealing with abuses, special guidelines should be developed and adopted.

Nations often impose PERFORMANCE REQUIREMENTS on foreign-controlled companies operating in their territory. These can include minimum export levels or domestic-content requirements. New provisions for performance requirements should be negotiated to reduce those that are damaging to other countries' interests.

More effective international coordination of domestic macroeconomic policies is needed to achieve better EXCHANGE RATE EQUILIBRIUM, and International Monetary Fund (IMF) surveillance of the industrial countries' exchange rates should be strengthened. With respect to the dollar-yen exchange rate, the yen should be strengthened by further Japanese liberalization of capital inflows and encouagement of its use as an international reserve currency.

The tax treatment of imports and exports as they enter and leave countries has long been a source of dispute among trading nations. This issue should be the subject of a comprehensive study by the U.S government. Until such a study is complete and agreement on this issue is reached with our trading partners the U.S. government should continue export tax benefits through the an equivalent replacement to the Domestic International Sales Corporation (DISC).

6. Trade in Services

We urge this country to take the lead in reducing restrictions and establishing a stable environment for the growing international trade in services. A major goal should be the development of an INTERNATIONAL SYSTEM for service trade and a means of settling disputes in this area.

As a first step, the United States should review its own laws and regulations and revise those that discourage service exports.

A midterm goal should be the establishment of a non-rule-making international body (preferably within GATT) to exchange information, settle disputes, and discourage new restrictions on service trade. The ultimate goal of these international negotiations should be to reduce barriers to service trade and to establish some international guidelines at the GATT level to govern this sector of commerce.

NOTES

1. A statement by the Research and Policy Committee of the Committee for Economic Development.

2. See Productivity Policy: Key to the Nation's Economic Future (1983). Competitiveness will be improved only if productivity growth is consistently higher than in the past. Short-term improvements during the early stage of an economic recovery are not sufficient for restoring competitiveness. During the first year of the recovery from the 1981-82 recession, manufacturing productivity growth was somewhat higher than during recoveries from most previous recessions. But for the private business sector as a whole the improvement was less than the improvement for all recessions since World War II.

3. For a review of the major industrial policies, see William F. Baumol and Kenneth McLennan, eds., Stimulation of U.S. Productivity Growth (New York: Oxford University Press, forthcoming 1984), Chapter 8.

4. See George C. Eads, "The Political Experience in Allocating Investment: Lessons from the United States and Elsewhere," in Toward a New U.S. Industrial Policy?, eds., Michael L. Wachter and and Susan M. Wachter (Philadelphia: University of Pennsylvania Press, 1981), pp. 453-482. For an empirical estimate of the contribution to productivity growth through resource reallocation by the market system, see Frank Gollop, "Evidence for a Sector-Biased or Sector-Neutral Industrial Strategy: Analysis of the Productivity Slowdown," in Stimulation of U.S. Productivity Growth, eds., Baumol and McLennan.

5. Organization for Economic Cooperation and Development Council at Ministerial Level, Positive Adjustment Policies: Managing Structural Change (Paris: Organization for Economic Cooperation and Development, 1982), p. 2.

6. For a more detailed review of actions management and labor can take to improve competitiveness, see "What Management and Labor Can Do" in the policy statement Productivity Policy: Key to the Nation's Economic Future (1983), Chapter 6.

7. For a complete discussion of the conditions under which markets do not work perfectly and the criteria for selecting the form of government intervention, see the policy statement Redefining Government's Role in the Market System (1979), Chapter 6.

8. See Appendix of this complete study for a table describing the possible results of policy strategies designed to strengthen the market economy and correct market weaknesses.

9. See Stimulating Technological Progress (1980) and Productivity Policy: Key to the Nation's Economic Future (1983).

Excerpted from Strategy for U.S. Industrial Competitiveness, A Statement by the Research and Policy Committee of the Committee for Economic Development, April 1984. Reprinted by permission of the Committee for Economic Development.

Conclusion

*Thomas E. Petri, William F. Clinger, Jr.,
Nancy L. Johnson, and Lynn Martin*

The United States does not need an industrial policy. The growth of our productivity and industrial capacity did slow between the sixties and the current recovery. But the government itself caused much of the problem. Government policies discouraged enterprise and distorted our market economy. High taxes, burdensome regulations, and government absorption of capital have hurt industry badly. Yet advocates of industrial policy propose even more government intervention and subsidies as the solutions to our problems.

A national industrial policy rests on the assumption that the government is somehow more adept than citizens at investing capital and choosing successful industries. But there are no abstract criteria by which the government can choose the industries and businesses that will thrive, or identify the lines and products in which our country will be most successful. The American economy has been the most successful and creative economy in history because, among its attributes, it allows individuals to spend and invest their own money, businessmen to manage their own industries, and capital markets to move resources in the best direction.

Even if government planning could somehow manage an economy more efficiently than market forces, our own political system is certainly incapable of doing so. The Founding Fathers created a government with many checks and balances and many centers of power, sacrificing efficiency to achieve wide participation and support for decisions when finally made. Such a government should not try to discriminate in favor of certain businesses, certain regions of the country, or certain groups of workers. That kind of effort will inevitably become bloated and costly, distributing subsidies to all those adept at winning favors.

Some advocates point to changes in the American economy as proof that we need a national industrial policy. But change is the inevitable consequence of a dynamic economy. We should try to ensure that change will be beneficial and productive, and not try to stifle it by freezing ourselves in our old ways. In fact, the strength of the American system has traditionally been its adaptability, its willingness to reward innovation and reject attempts to inhibit market forces.

Further, it is not true that the United States is "deindustrializing." From 1960 to 1980 there was not only no decline in the percentage of gross national product originating in the manufacturing sector, but there was an increase. In the 1970s the United States increased its employment in manufacturing more rapidly than any other major industrialized nation, and total employment grew by 24%. From 1950 to 1980 overall industrial production increased nearly 300%.

Our economy has shown itself to be remarkably flexible, moving resources into areas where we perform best. Some industries have declined and some workers have lost their jobs. But many more businesses have started up, and new workers are joining the workforce every day. Our government should try to ease the pain of dislocated workers. But it shouldn't forbid change that will create more new jobs than are lost.

The debate over industrial policy need not be conducted in a vacuum. Other nations have instituted many of the steps proposed by industrial policy advocates. The results have been dismal. The German post-war miracle has been tarnished by recent government interventions in its market economy. Great Britain's economy was almost suffocated by a mass of protective measures, subsidies, industry nationalizations, and costly loans to inefficient businesses.

Japan and its Ministry of International Trade and Industry (MITI) are often cited as examples of successful government planning and action. But Japan's success has not resulted from a government-adopted national industrial policy, but from an exceptionally free and entrepreneurial economy. Taxes have been low, savings and capital formation have been encouraged, workers typically have been given a stake in productivity improvement, and Japanese businesses have responded with efficiency admired throughout the world. To the extent the Japanese government has involved itself in allocating resources, it has tended to do so as directed by industry groups rather than as the director of industries—an important distinction glossed over by American industrial policy advocates.

Valuable lessons on industrial policy can be found in our own nation's history as well. For example, our government's investment in research and development has been most successful when it created a framework where scientific and user interests could guide allocation. It has failed when the government has tried to identify projects that would be winners in market competition.

We believe a national industrial policy would be disastrous for this nation. But our message is not only negative. There are steps we can take to improve the performance of our economy. Our goal should be to make our market economy operate as fairly and efficiently as possible, and for the benefit of all Americans, rather than discriminating among firms and industries. For example, we must get the Federal government out of the credit markets where it competes with private sector borrowing and raises the cost of capital; we must slow the growth of government expenditures; we must reform the tax code to remove disincentives to savings and capital investment; we must continually review government regulations to determine their effect on economic growth and competition; we must revise our antitrust laws to allow more cooperation in research and development; and we must work to eliminate barriers to foreign trade.

Our work is cut out for us. Yet, with proper measures, we can make our country and all its inhabitants more prosperous. But we must remember that we don't need centralized government planning. And we don't need a misguided and dangerous national industrial policy.

About the Contributors

WILLIAM H. BRANSON is a Professor of Economics and International Affairs at the Woodrow Wilson School, Princeton University.

JOHN BURTON is a Research Fellow with the Institute of Economic Affairs in London, England.

PAT CHOATE is a Senior Policy Analyst at T.R.W., Inc. in Washington, D.C. He is author of the forthcoming book, Working Ahead, and is co-author of America in Ruins: the Deteriorating Infrastructure (Duke University Press) and Being Number One: Rebuilding the U.S. Economy (Lexington Books).

RICHARD N. LANGLOIS is Assistant Professor of Economics at the University of Connecticut in Storrs, Connecticut.

ROBERT Z. LAWRENCE is a Senior Fellow at the Brookings Institution. He is the author of Can America Compete? (Brookings), Commodity Prices and the New Inflation (Brookings), and numerous other studies in International Economics.

RICHARD B. McKENZIE teaches economics at Clemson University and is an adjunct scholar at the Heritage Foundation.

RICHARD R. NELSON is a Professor of Economics at Yale University, New Haven, Connecticut.

KLAUS-DIETER SCHMIDT is with the Institute for World Economics in Kiel, West Germany.

PHILIP H. TREZISE is a Senior Fellow at the Brookings Institution and is a former Assistant Secretary of State for Economic Affairs.

CHARLES L. SCHULTZE is a Senior Fellow in the Economics Studies Program at the Brookings Institution. He was Chairman of the President's Council of Economic Advisers from 1977-1980 and Director of the U.S. Bureau of the Budget from 1965-1967. His books include The Public Use of Private Interest.

JOHN A. YOUNG is President and Chief Executive Officer of Hewlett-Packard Company and is serving as Chairman of the President's Commission on Industrial Competitiveness.

Bibliography

I. THE DEBATE DEFINED

Badaracco, Joseph L., Jr., and David B. Yoffie. "Industrial Policy": it can't happen here. Harvard business review, v. 106, Nov-Dec. 1983: 97-105.

Bartlett, Bruce, and Kent Hughes. Does the United States need an industrial policy? Policy report, v. 5, Nov. 1983: 5-9.

Eismeier, Theodore J. The case against industrial policy. Journal of contemporary studies, v. 6, spring 1983: 17-27.

Industrial policy debate. New York, WNET/Thirteen, 1983. 8 p. The MacNeil-Lehrer report, July 14, 1983.

Industrial policy: is it the answer? Business week, no. 2797, July 4, 1983: 54-57, 61-62.

Lee, Dwight R. Robert Reich's industrial fantasies. Journal of contemporary studies, v. 6, summer 1983: 65-75.

Lekachman, Robert. The limitations of industrial policy. New leader, v. 66, Sept. 19, 1983: 5-7.

Levitt, Arthur, Jr., Industrial policy: slogan or solution? Harvard business review, v. 62, Mar.-Apr. 1984: 6-8.

Modic, Stanley J., Robert B. Reich, and Jerry J. Jasinowski. A U.S. industrial policy? Yes and no. Industry week, v. 219, Nov. 14, 1983: 38-40, 42-44.

The Political realities of industrial policy. Harvard business review, v. 61, Sept.-Oct. 1983: 76-86.

Reich, Robert B. An industrial policy of the right. Public interest, no. 73, fall 1983: 3-17.

Reich, Robert B. Industrial evolution, Democracy, v. 3, summer 1983: 10-20.

Rohatyn, Felix G. A case for reindustrialization: an interview with Felix G. Rohatyn. Forbes, v. 133, Jan. 30, 1984: 54-55, 58-59.

Schwartz, Elliot. The industrial policy debate. Washington, U.S. Congressional Budget office, for sale by the Supt. of Docs., 1983. 22, 70p.

Stein, Herbert. Don't fall for industrial policy. Fortune, v. 108, Nov. 14, 1983: 64-66, 70, 74, 78.

II. THE LESSONS OF EXPERIENCE

Carlsson, Bo. Industrial subsidies in Sweden: macro-economic effects and an international comparison. Journal of industrial economics, v. 32, Sept. 1983: 1-23.

Denzau, Arthur T., A national development bank: ghost of the RFC past. St. Louis Center for the Study of American Business, 1984. 21 p.

Donges, Juergen B. Industrial policies in West Germany's not so market-oriented economy. World economy, v. 3, Sept. 1980: 185-204.

Estrin, Saul, and Peter Holmes. French planning and industrial policy. Journal of public policy, v. 3, Feb. 1983: 131-148.

Faini, Riccardo. Regional implications of industrial policy: the Italian case. Journal of public policy, v. 3, Feb. 1983: 97-118.

Franko, Lawrence G. Industrial policies in Western Europe—solution or problem? World economy, v. 2, Jan. 1979: 31-50.

Gall, Norman. The rise and decline of industrial Japan. Commentary, v. 76, Oct. 1983: 27-34.

Girvin, Brian. Irish industrial policy: the constraints and opportunities of an open economy. Journal of public policy, v. 3, Feb. 1983: 81-96.

Grant, R.M. Appraising selective financial assistance to industry: a review of institutions and methodologies in the United Kingdom, Sweden and West Germany. Journal of public policy, v. 3, Oct. 1983: 369-396.

Grant, Wyn. British Industrial policy: structural change, policy inertia. Journal of public policy, v. 3 Feb. 1983: 13-28.

Green, Diana. Promoting the industries of the future: the search for an industrial strategy in Britain and France. Journal of public policy, v. 1, Aug. 1981: 333-351.

Hadley, Eleanor M. The secret of Japan's success. Challenge, v. 26, May-June 1983: 4-10.

Hesselman, Linda. Trends in European industrial intervention. Cambridge journal of economics, v. 7, June 1983: 197-208.

Hills, Jill. The industrial policy of Japan. Journal of public policy, v. 3, Feb. 1983: 63-80.

Lincoln, Edward J. Japan's industrial policies; what are they, do they matter and are they different from those in the United States? Washington, Japan Economic Institute of America, 1984. 56p.

McKay, David, and Wyn Grant. Industrial policies in OECD countries: an overview. Journal of public policy, v. 3, Feb. 1983: 1-12.

Muller, Wolfgang C. Economic success without an industrial policy: Austria in the 1970s. Journal of public policy, v. 3, Feb. 1983: 119-130.

Schmitt, Roland W. National R&D policy: industrial perspective. Science, v. 224, June 15, 1984: 1206-1209.

Sidenius, Niels. Danish industrial policy: persistent liberalism. Journal of public policy, v. 3, Feb. 1983: 49-62.

Spencer, Edson W. Japan: stimulus or scapegoat? Foreign affairs, v. 62, fall 1983: 123-137.

Taira, Koji. Industrial policy and employment in Japan. Current history, v. 82, Nov. 1983: 362-365, 392-393.

Tanaka, H. William, and B. Jenkins Middleton. Injured industries, imports and industrial policy: a comparison of United States and Japanese practices. Journal of international law, v. 15, summer 1983: 419-443.

Tsuruta, Toshimasa. The myth of Japan, Inc. Technology review, v. 86, July 1983: 43-48.

III. CHANGING ECONOMIC STRUCTURE

Academy for State and Local Government. Contrasting approaches to economic growth: the national industrial policy debate and State and local economic development strategy. Washington, D.C., The Academy, 1984. 45p.

Miller, James C., III. Reindustrialization policy: Atari mercantilism? Policy report, v. 5, July 1983: 1, 3-5.

Mutti, John, and Peter Morici. Changing petterns of U.S. industrial activity and comparative advantage. Washington, D.C., National Planning Association, Committee on Changing International Realities, 1983. 64 p. (CIR report no. 14, NPA report no. 201).

IV. POLICY RECOMMENDATIONS

AFL-CIO, Industrial Union Department. Deindustrialization and the two-tier society. Washington, D.C. 1984.

AmeriTrust Corporation. Choosing a future: Steps to revitalize the mid-American economy. 1984.

Blumenthal, Sidney. Drafting a Democratic industrial plan. New York times magazine, Aug. 28, 1983: 31, 40-48, 53, 56-59, 63.

Business-Higher Education Forum. America's competitive challenge: The need for a national response. 1983.

The Business Roundtable. Analysis of the issues in the national industrial policy debate. Washington, D.C. May 1984.

Center for Strategic and International Studies, Georgetown University. U.S. strategies and foreign industrial targeting. Washington, D.C. 1982.

Chamber of Commerce of the United States. A national export policy: Recommendations for expanding U.S. exports. Washington, D.C. 1982.

Computer and Business Equipment Manufacturers Association. Industrial policy: A position statement. Washington, D.C. September 1983.

Congressional Budget Office. The productivity problem: Alternatives for action. Washington, D.C. 1981.

Congressional Budget Office. Federal support for r&d and innovation. Washington, D.C. April 1984.

Data Resources, Inc. The DRI report on U.S. manufacturing industries. McGraw Hill. 1983.

Etzioni, Amitai. American industrial policy: the MITIzation of America? Public interest, no. 72, summer 1983: 44-51.

Gilder, George. American industrial policy: a supply-side economics of the left. Public interest, no. 72, summer 1983: 29-43.

Heritage Foundation. A blueprint for jobs and industrial growth. Washington, D.C. 1983.

House Republican Research Committee Task Force on High Technology. An agenda for U.S. technological leadership and industrial competitiveness. Washington, D.C. 1984.

House Wednesday Group. Human capital and national economic development. Washington, D.C. July 1983. 19p.

House Wednesday Group. U.S. economic infrastructure. Washington, D.C. May 1982. 17p.

Joint Economic Committee. U.S. Congress. Industrial policy movement in the United States: is it the answer? A staff study prepared for the use of the Joint Economic Committee, Congress of the United States. Washington, D.C., G.P.O., 1984. 102p.

Kaus, Robert M. Can creeping socialism cure creeping capitalism? Harper's, v. 266, Feb. 1983: 17-22.

Labor-Industry Coalition for International Trade. International trade, industrial policies, and the future of American industry. Washington, D.C. 1983.

National Association of Manufacturers. Agenda for regaining America's initiative. Washington, D.C. 1983.

National Commission on Excellence in Education. A nation at risk: The imperative for educational reform. Washington, D.C. 1983.

National Research Council, National Academy of Sciences. International competition in advanced technology, decisions for America. Washington, D.C. 1983.

Senate Democratic Policy Committee. Jobs for the future: A Democratic agenda. Washington, D.C. November 1983.

Senate Republican Conference. Report and recommendations. Washington, D.C. 1984.

U.S. Congress, Senate Committee on Finance. Future of U.S. basic industries. Hearings, 98th Congress, 1st session. Washington, G.P.O., 1984. 430p.

U.S. Department of Commerce. Conference on new climate for joint research. Washington, D.C. 1983.

U.S. Department of Commerce. Report to the President from the Secretary of Commerce. Washington, D.C. 1984.

U.S. Department of Commerce. The Stevenson-Wydler technology innovation act of 1980. Washington, D.C. 1980

Weidenbaum, Murray L. Industrial policy is not the answer. Challenge, v. 26, July-Aug. 1983: 22-25.

White House Conference on Productivity. Productivity growth: A better life for America. Washington, D.C. 1984.

Index

Administrative Procedures Act, 19
Agriculture, 54, 55, 58, 59, 61, 90, 92, 93, 102, 117, 126-127
  Aircraft industry, 85, 88, 90
American competitiveness strategy. See Competitiveness
American Trust Corporation, 133
Anti-trust, 128, 130, 155
  laws, 137
  policy, 99
Auto industry, 34, 42, 49, 74, 77, 78, 85, 117, 121-122, 126
  Japanese auto industry, 59-61

Badaracco, Joseph, 31, 32
Bank for Industrial Competitiveness, 134
Bankruptcy, 35, 65, 74
Benn, Tony, 77
Bluestone, Barry, 27, 28, 40
Bomberg, Howard, ix
Brandt, Chancellor Willy, 64
Branson, William H., 98, 115, 163
Brazil, 119
British Leyland, 49, 74, 77, 79, 81
British Motor Company (BMC), 74
Budget deficits, 21, 22, 37, 38, 122, 134, 152

Bundesverband der Industrie (BDI), 68
Burton, John, 49, 71, 163
Business cycle, 4, 10, 39
Business-Higher Education Forum, 128, 133
Business Roundtable, 133

Canada, 10, 97
Capacity utilization, 104
Capital, 8, 10, 12, 15, 17, 22, 27, 40, 53, 129
  formation, 109, 135
Chile, 119
Choate, Pat, 98, 125, 163
Chrysler, 34, 35, 136
Clarke, Christina, ix
Clinger, William, viii, ix, 3, 159
Coal mining industry, 49, 64, 65, 66, 68, 125
  West Germany, 64, 66
Cohen, Ben, ix
Committee for Economic Development, 128, 133, 147
Comparative advantage, 15, 16, 42, 43, 44, 98, 102, 116-122
Competition, international, 102, 139 See also Competitiveness
Competitiveness, 3, 4, 5, 7, 8, 27, 31, 36, 42, 127, 128-130, 134, 138, 139, 140, 144, 147, 148. See also Comparative advantage or Competition, international

171

Computer and business equipment manufacturers, 133
Computers, 32, 37, 85, 90. See also High-tech
Concorde, 76, 81, 94, 140
Congressional Budget Office, 133
Consumption bids, 149
Cook, Matt, ix
Cooperative Automative Research Generic Technologies Program (COGENT), 91
Coordination, 19, 20, 27, 44
Council on Industrial Competition, 134
Credit, 134
Crowding out, 149

Data Resources, Inc., 133
Defense, 17, 39, 41, 89, 122
Deficit, 112, 117, 121, 122, 134
  trade, 116, 140
Deindustrialization, 1, 3, 7, 9, 10, 11, 14, 23, 27, 97, 101-113, 115-123, 148
Department of Commerce, 133
Department of Economic Affairs (DEA), 74
Deregulation, 135, 136
Deutsche mark, 63
Devaluation, 4, 112, 118
Developing countries, 116, 120
Dislocation of workers. See Worker Displacement
Dollar, 10, 17, 20, 101, 104, 116, 117, 122, 134, 138

Economic Cooperation Council. See Reconstruction Finance Corporation (RFC)
Economic Development Administration, 18
Economic Planning Agency, 60
Education, 8, 9, 27, 33, 54-55, 135, 137. See also Retraining
Edwardes, Sir Michael, 79
Elastic demand, 102
Employee Stock Ownership Plans (ESOP), 135
Employment, 10, 28, 29, 30, 31, 32, 33, 34, 38, 39,

Employment (continued)
40, 101, 102, 104, 108, 125, 126, 148
Energy, 54, 58, 98, 116, 117, 126
European Economic Community (EEC), 65
Exchange rate, 111, 153, 155
Export, 4, 8, 10, 15, 17, 22, 40, 43, 44, 101, 103, 104 116, 119, 120, 127
Export-Import Bank of Japan, 38, 56

Federal Financing Bank, 135
Federal Reserve, 21
Federal Trade Commission (FTC), 58
Feldstein, Martin, 122
Fiscal Investment and Loan Program (FILP), 12, 37, 56
Fiscal policy, 152
Fishing industry, 20
Flader, Joe, ix
Flexible exchange rate. See Exchange rate
Flexible-system production, 27
France, 80, 81, 86, 108, 109-111

General Agreement on Tariffs and Trade (GATT), 155
Georgetown University Center for Strategic and International Studies, 133
Germany. See West Germany
Gobron, Louise, ix
Great Britain. See United Kingdom
Gross domestic product (GDP), 107
Gross national product, 10, 11, 12, 14, 20, 28, 54, 86, 103, 106, 108, 111, 125, 136
Grylls, M., 78

Hager, Wolfgang, 42, 43
Harrison, Bennett, 27, 28
Hart, Gary, 32, 40
Health care, 136

Heath, Edward, 76, 77
Heritage Foundation, 133, 135
Hickle, James, 35, 36
High-tech, 1, 11, 19, 30, 42, 72, 97, 98, 102, 113, 116, 117, 120, 125, 127, 137, 153. See also Computers
Honda, 38
Hong Kong, 42
House Republican Research Committee Task Force on High Technology, 133
House Wednesday Group, ix, 133
Howaldtswerk, 67
Human capital, 119

Iaccoca, Lee, 36
Import restrictions. See Trade protection
Individual Retirement Account (IRA), 135
Industrial Development Advisory Board (IDAB), 77, 150
Industrial Expansion Act of 1978, 76
Industrial Reorganization Corporation (IRC), 74, 75, 78
Industrial Union Department 133
Industrial Unit (IDU), 77
Industry Act
 of 1972, 77
 of 1975, 78-80
Inflation, 6, 21, 29, 107, 129
Infrastructure, 27, 128, 135, 136
Interest rates, 21, 22, 116, 122, 134, 144
International Computer Limited, 75
International Monetary Fund (IMF), 104
Intra-industry trade, 15
Investment, 8, 16, 28, 101, 107, 109, 135, 149
Italy, 10, 42, 81, 97

Japan, 8, 9, 10, 12, 13, 32, 36, 38, 39, 40, 49, 50, 53-61, 67, 71, 80, 81, 86, 86, 108-109, 116, 126-127,

Japan (continued)
 138
Japan Defense Agency, 60
Japanese Development Bank (JDB), 13, 38, 53, 56, 57
Japanese Ministry of International Trade and Industry. See MITI
Japan National Railway, 37
Jefferson, Edward, 28
Job Training Partnership Act, 137
Johnson Administration, 18, 71
Johnson, Chalmers, 36, 43
Johnson, Nancy L. viii, ix, 49, 159
Joint Economic Committee, 133

Kennedy,
 and Tokyo Rounds, 64
 and Johnson years, 71
Keynesianism, 71, 128
Korea, 42
Krugman, Paul, 14, 16
Kuwait, 119

Labor, 33, 101, 106, 119, 133, 135, 137. See also Workers
Labor-Industry Coalition for International Trade (LICIT), 133
Labor Party of Great Britain, 74, 77
LaFalce, John, 32, 134
Laissez-faire, 107
Lame-duck policy, 76, 77
Langlois, Richard, 50, 85, 163
Lawrence, Robert, 97, 101, 163
Lincoln, Abraham, 127
Lindbeck, Assar, 16
Lockheed, 77
Losch, August, 68
Low-tech, 121, 123

Macroeconomic, 7, 8, 12, 20, 22, 94, 98, 99, 116, 123, 127, 134
Martin, Lynn, viii, ix, 97, 159
Maskus, Keith, 120
Mayers, Peter, ix

McKenzie, Richard B., 27, 163
McNaught, Fran, ix
Mergers, 66, 74
Microeconomics, 23, 99, 128, 130
MITI (Japanese Ministry of International Trade and Industry), 14, 36, 55, 58, 59
Model cities program, 18, 19
Mondale, Walter, 34
Monoyios, Nicholas, 119

National Academy of Sciences, 133
National Advisory Commission on Aeronautics (NACA), 91
National Aeronautic and Space Administration (NASA), 89, 90
National Association of Manufacturers, 133
National Commission on Excellence in Education, 133, 141
National Commission on Industrial Competitiveness, 131
National Economic Development Council (NEDC), 73
National Enterprise Board (NEB), 49, 78
Nationalization, 73
National Plan, 74
National Productivity Advisory Committee, 133
National Research Council, 133
Navigation Acts of 1651, 1660, 72
Nebraska, 126
Nelson, Richard R., 50, 85, 163
New Industrial Strategy, 78

Oil. See Energy
Olson, Mancur, 39
Operation Breakthrough, 93, 94

Packwood, Dave, 144
Pagel, Gretchen, ix
Patent law, 137
Patrick, Hugh, 13

Petri, Thomas, viii, ix, 1, 133, 159
Petroleum refining. See Energy
Pharmaceuticals industry, 85, 88, 90
Picking losers, 3, 99, 131
Picking winners, 3, 93, 99, 131
Planning agreement, 80
Policy peddler, 33
President's Commission on Industrial Competitiveness, 133, 140, 142, 145
Producer-provider, 88, 89
Product-cycle, 120
Productivity, 6, 10, 11, 12, 28, 33, 42, 73, 86, 97, 98, 99, 101, 102, 105, 106-111, 122, 129, 142
Protectionist. See Trade protection

Railroad, 54, 57
Randolph, Alfred M., Jr., ix
Reagan Administration, 27, 40,
Recession, 29, 101, 107
Reconstruction Finance Corporation (RFC), 13, 15, 19, 128
Redwood, J., 78
Regulatory rules, 98, 134, 136, 154
Reich, Robert, 27, 28, 36, 40, 42
Relative advantage. See Comparative advantage
Research and Development (R&D), 8, 20, 36, 37, 50, 54, 60, 75, 85-95, 97, 105, 109, 120, 137, 143, 144
Roberts, Susie, ix
Rohatyn, Felix, 72, 128
Rolls Royce, 77, 79
Roy, A. D., 110
Ruhrkohle, Ag, 66
Rural policy, 128
Ryder Plan, 78

Sakoh, Katsuro, 38
Samuelson, Robert, 33

Schlieker Shipyard, 67
Schmidt, Chancellor Helmut,
Schmidt, Klaus-Dieter, 49, 63, 163
Schultze, Charles, 3-8, 25, 163
Sector working parties (SWP), 79
Semiconductors, 85, 90. See also High-tech
Senate Democratic Policy Committee, 133, 134
Senate Republican Conference Study, 133, 138
Sherman Act, 58
Shipbuilding industry, 49, 58, 67, 107, 126
South Africa, 119
Soybeans, 43, 44
Status quo, 98
Steel industry, 19, 20, 29, 31, 42, 49, 55, 58, 65, 66-67, 107, 110, 121, 126
Stern, Robert, 120
Subsidies, 54, 87, 154, 156
Sunrise industries, 28, 72
Sunset industries, 71, 81
Supersonic transport (SST), 89, 93, 94
Supply-side economics, 7, 128

Tansey, Lori, ix
Tax, 41, 50, 55, 101, 123, 135
  code, 20, 22, 94, 152-153
Technical education. See Education
Textile industry, 19, 40, 41, 42, 43, 44, 55, 58, 79, 121, 126
Thatcher, Margaret, 73, 80, 81
Thurow, Lester, 28, 31, 36, 40
Timber industry, 20
Trade, 4, 10, 14, 21, 22, 32, 36, 39-41, 50, 102, 144
  protection, 17, 40, 57-58, 64, 68, 72, 115, 138, 155
Trezise, Philip, 13, 37, 38, 50, 53, 163
Tristar, 77

Unemployment, 6, 10, 22, 24, 28, 29, 30-31, 33, 41, 64, 111, 154
United Kingdom, 19, 24, 36, 38, 49, 51, 71-81, 108, 109
United States Trade Policy Council, 28
U.S.-Japan Advisory Commission, 144
Urban policy, 128
User-demander, 88

Van Der Meid, Ted, ix
Vereinigte Flutechnische, 66
Vernon, Raymond, 120

Wages, 33, 38, 39, 41, 42, 111, 119
Weirton plant, 19
West Germany, 10, 24, 37, 49, 51, 63-69, 80, 97, 108-111
West Midlands of England, 78
White-hot technological revolution, 74, 76
White House Council on Productivity, 133
Whitman, Marina, 121
Wool industry, 19. See also Textile industry
Workers, 16-18, 31, 32
  displacement of, 98, 112-113
  relocation of, 123
  retraining of, 8, 18, 115, 123, 130, 137

Yen, 43, 138
Young, John, 138, 139, 164
Youngstown plant, 19